Letters to My Baby Boy

New Mommy Journal

This book is for

____

Born

____

Love,

Mommy

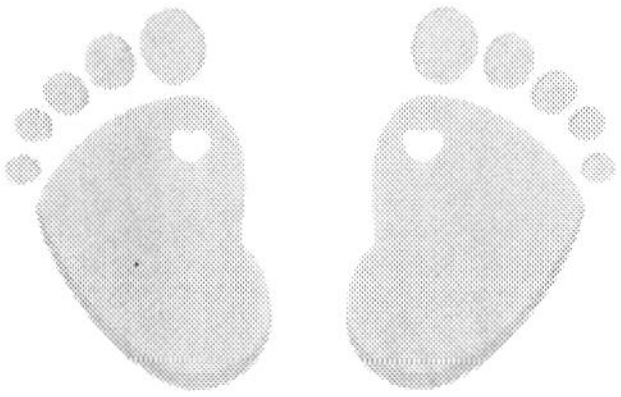

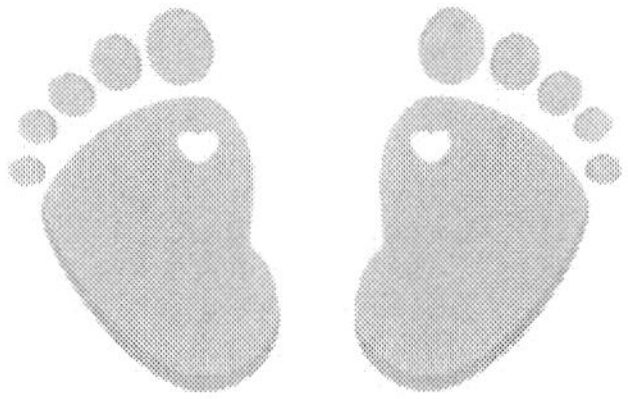

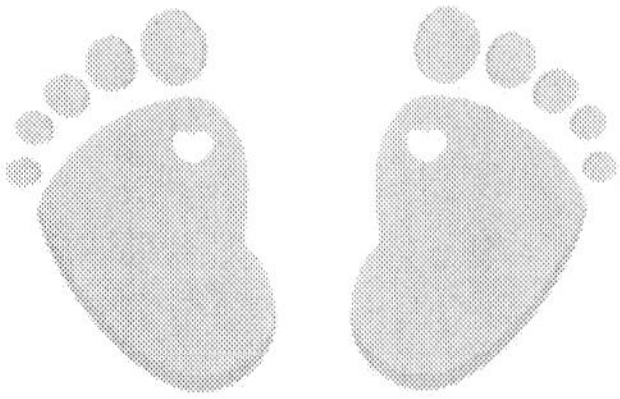

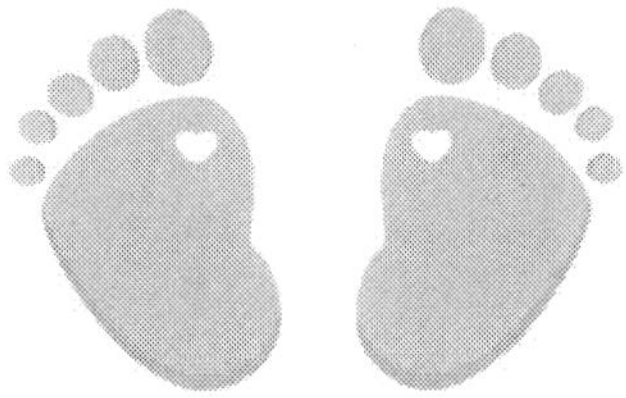

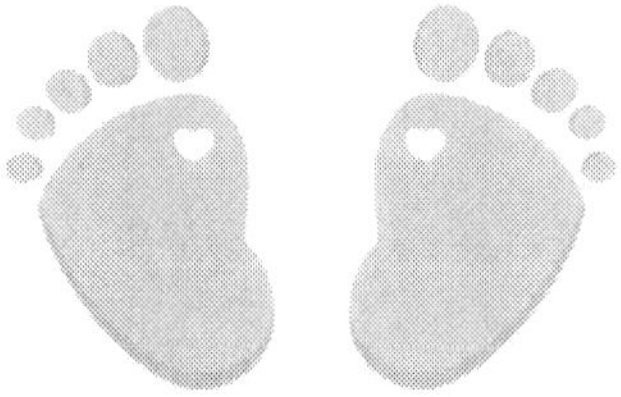

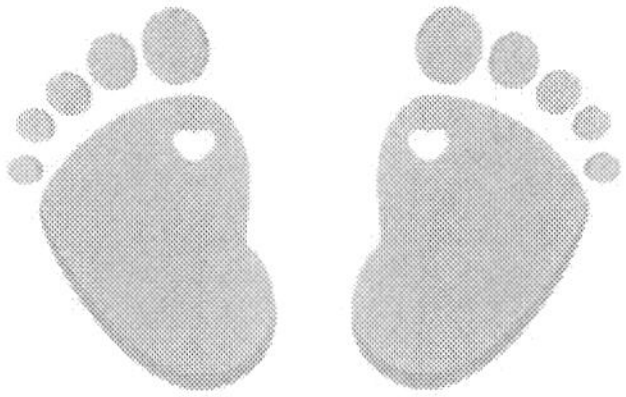

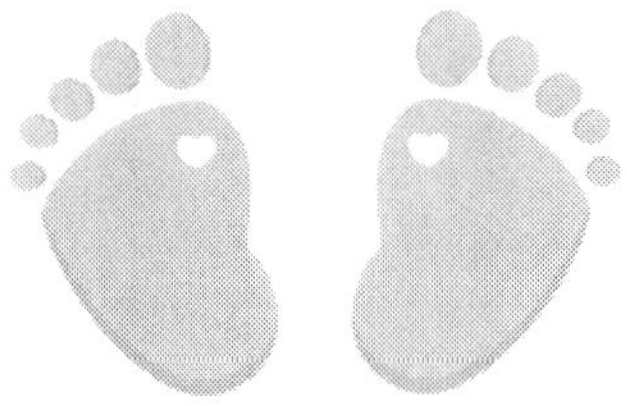

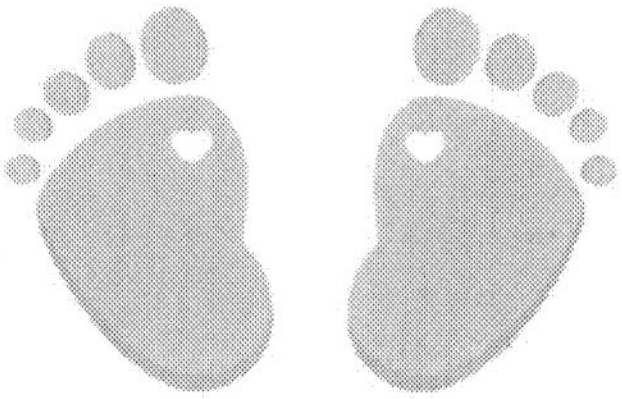

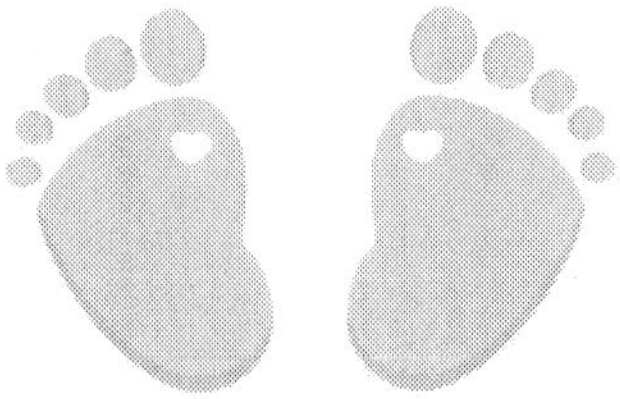

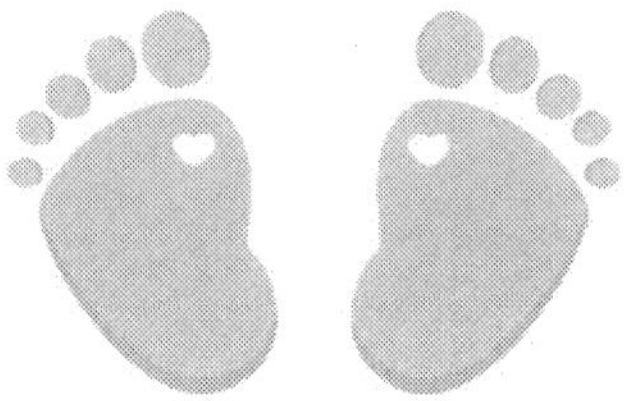

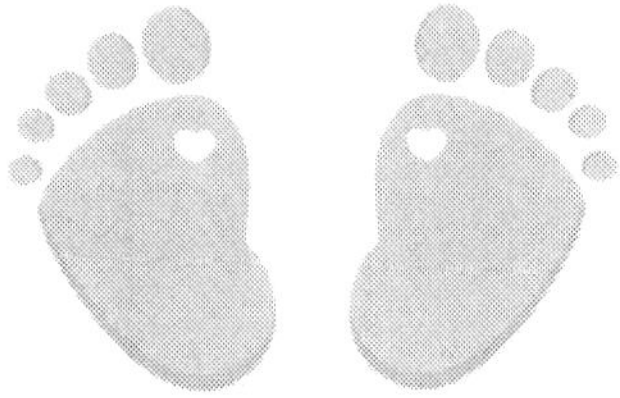

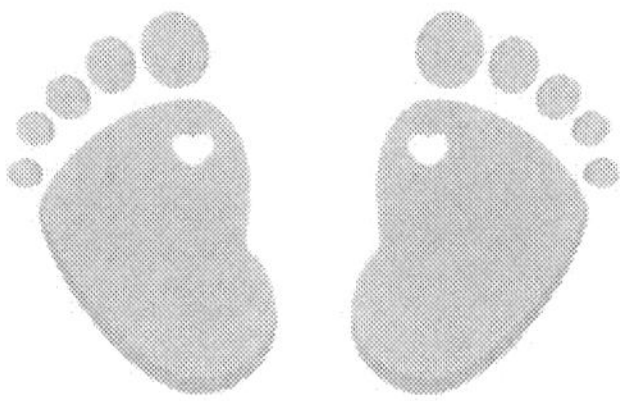

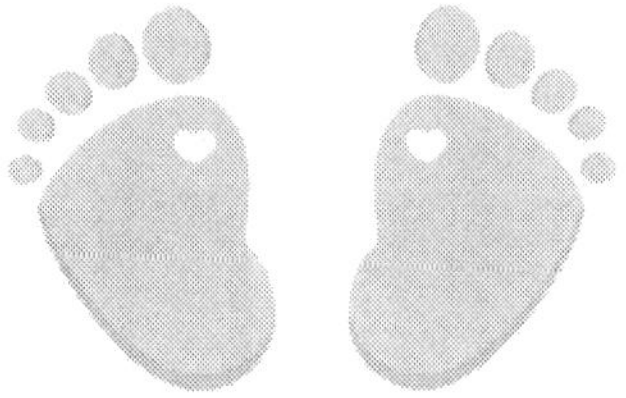

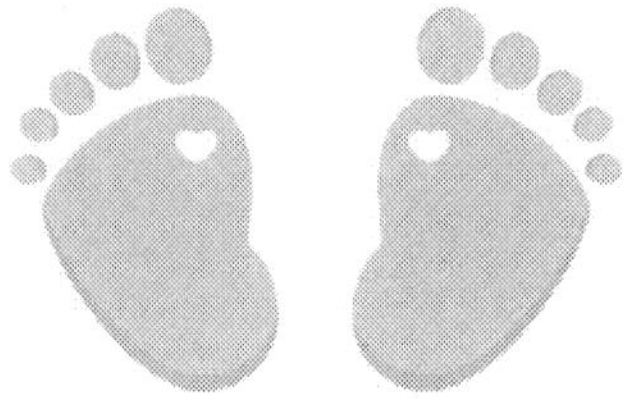

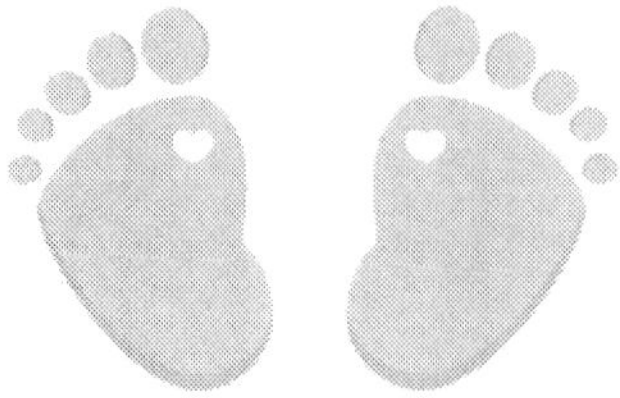

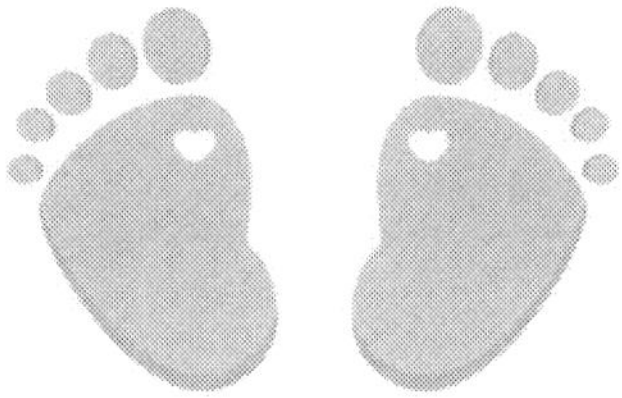

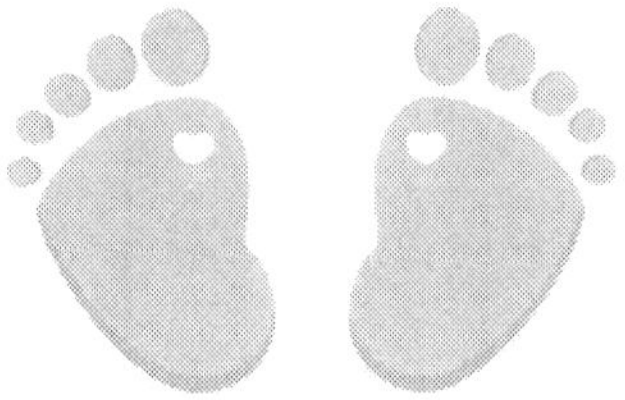

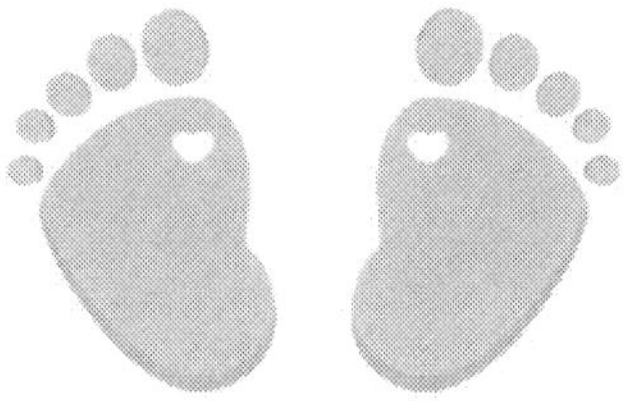

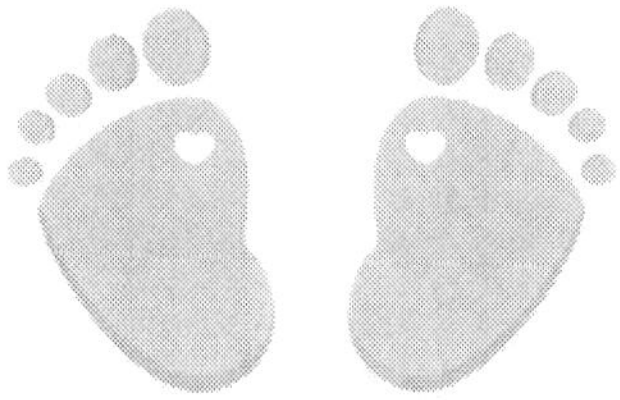

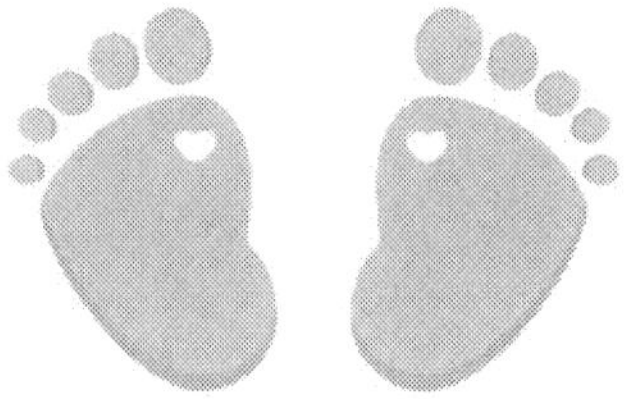

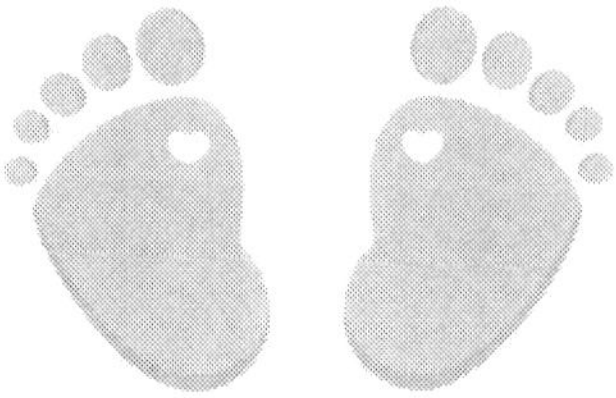

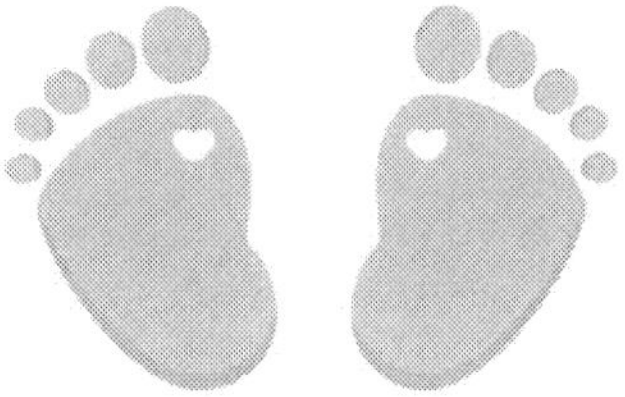

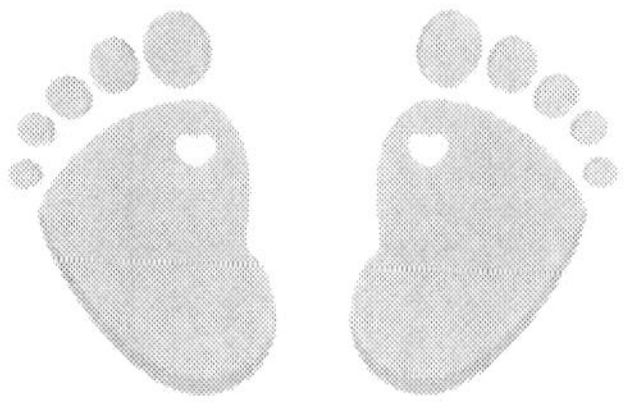

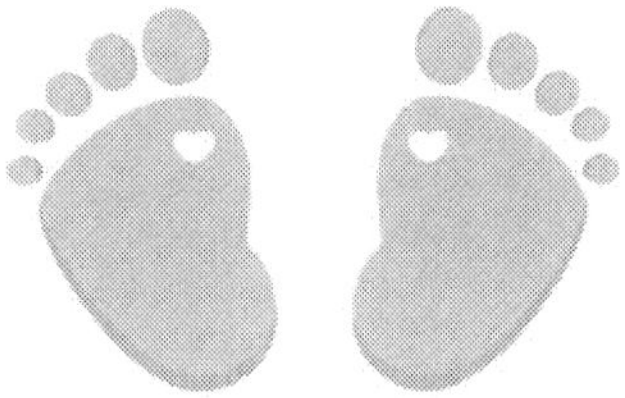

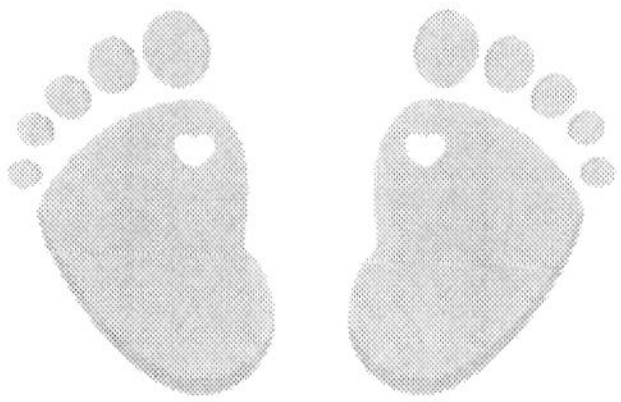

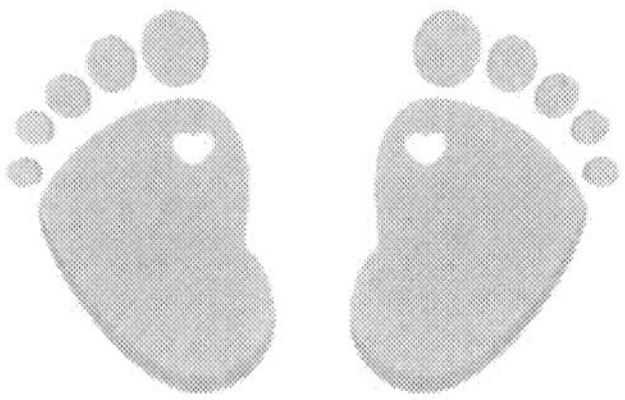

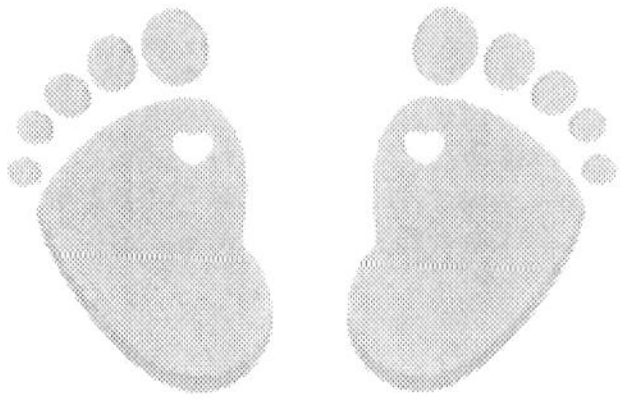

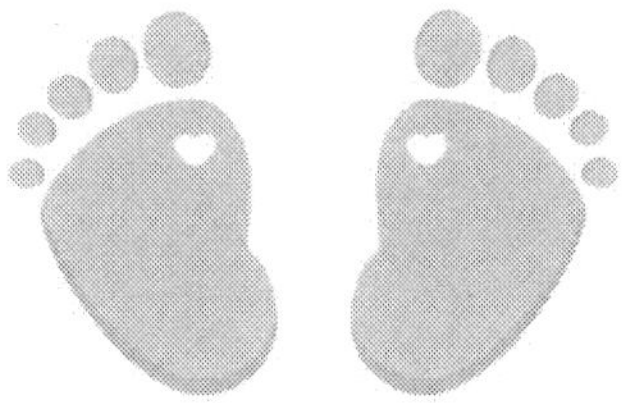

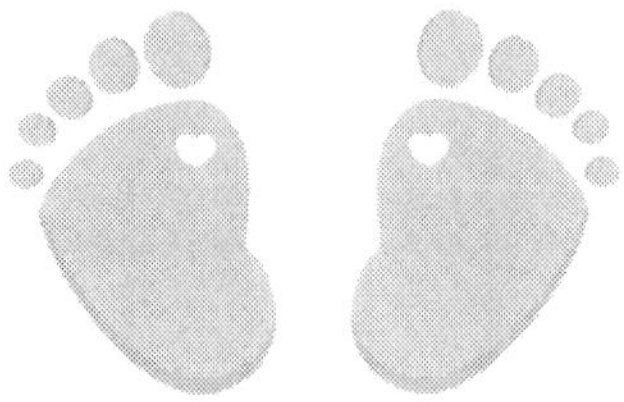

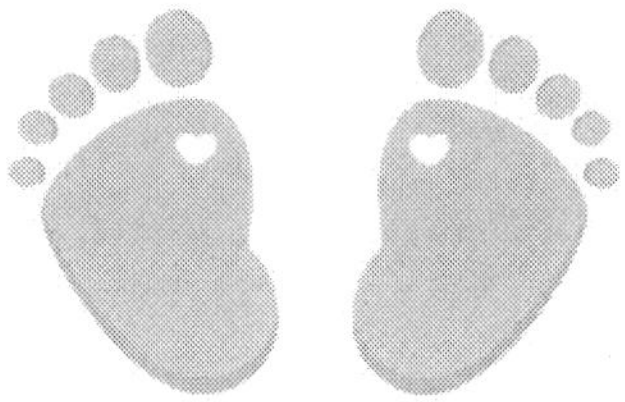

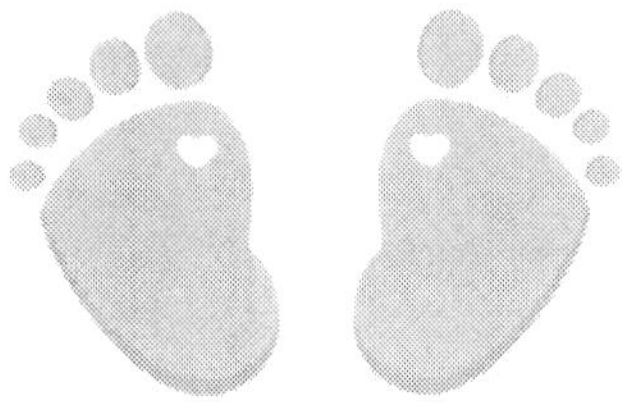

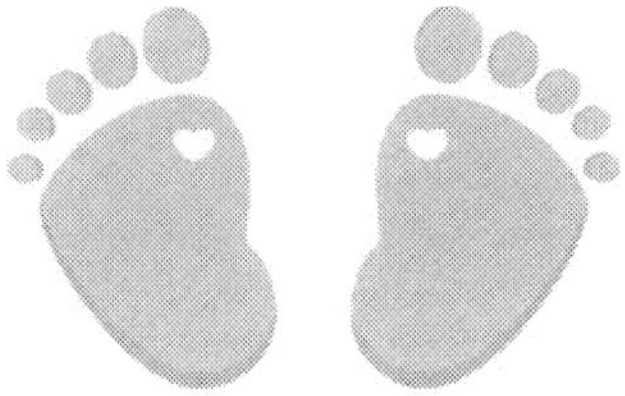

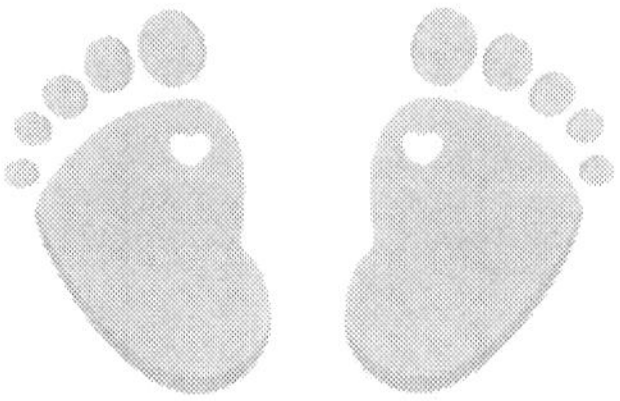

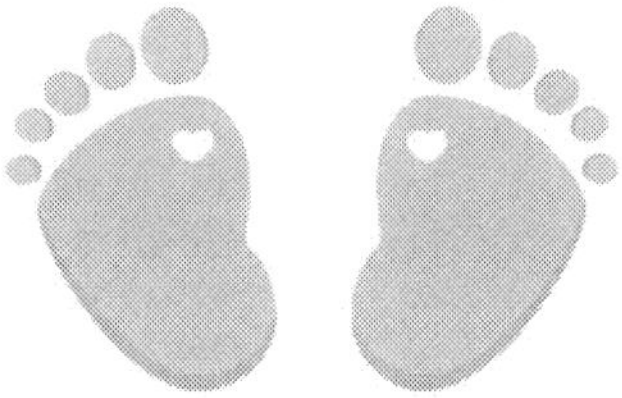

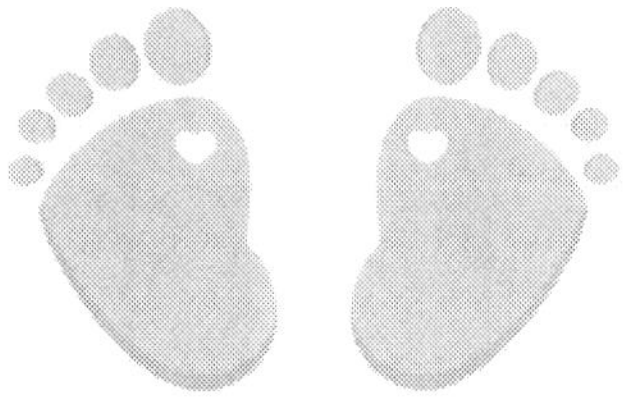

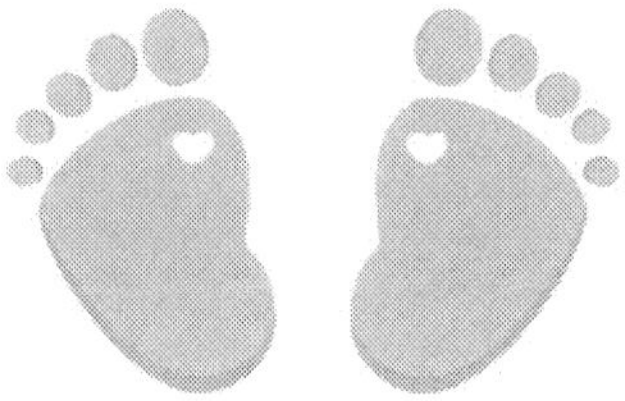

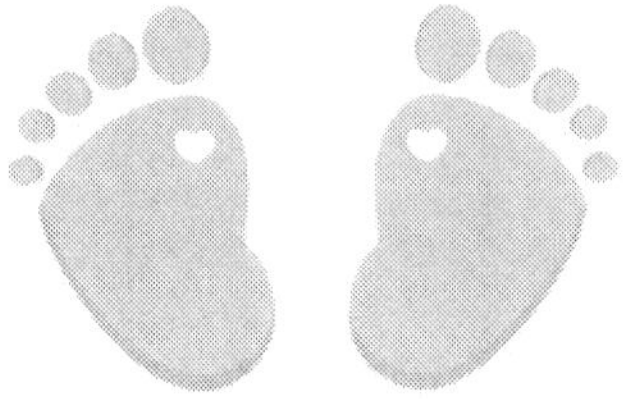

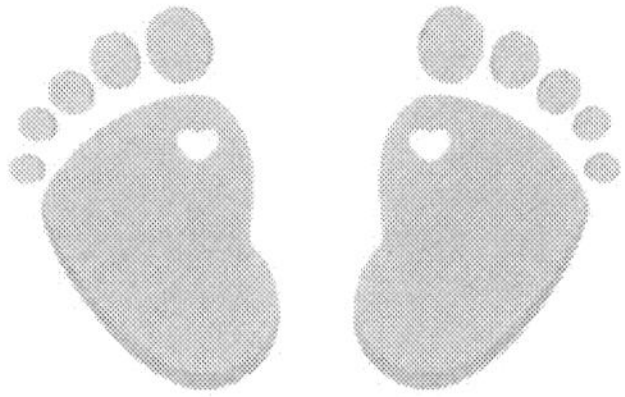

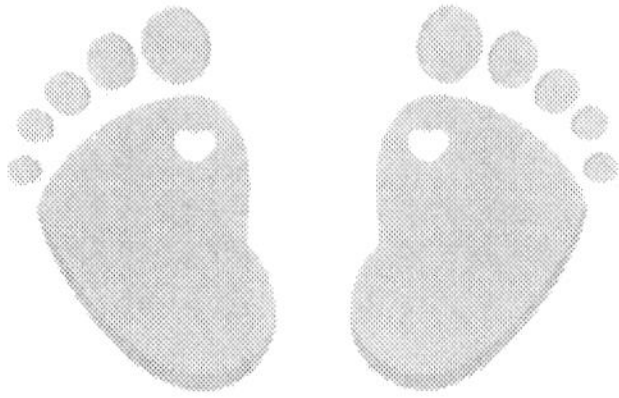

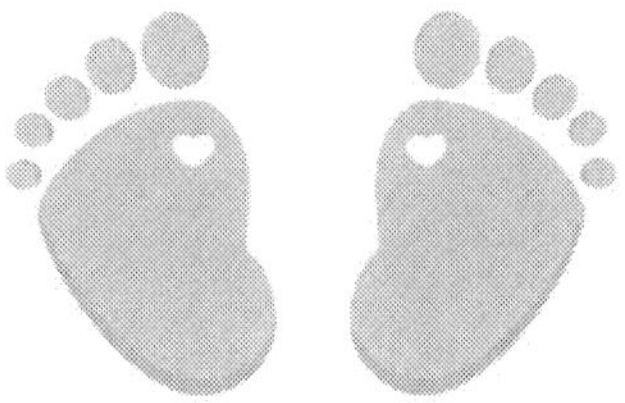

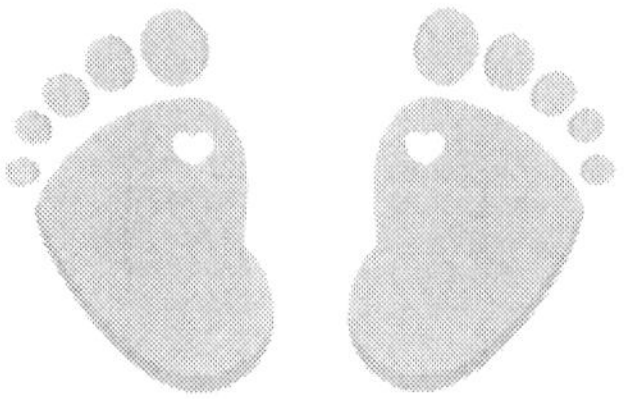

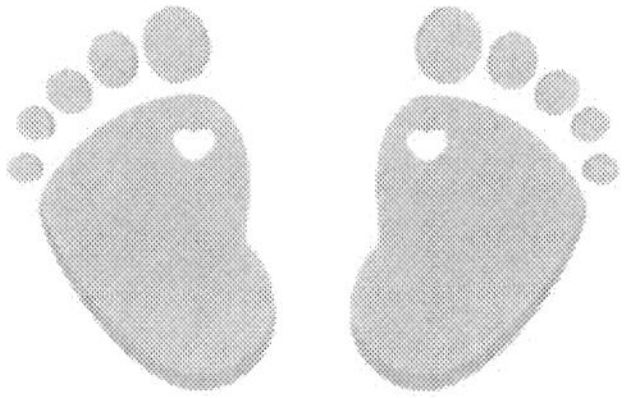

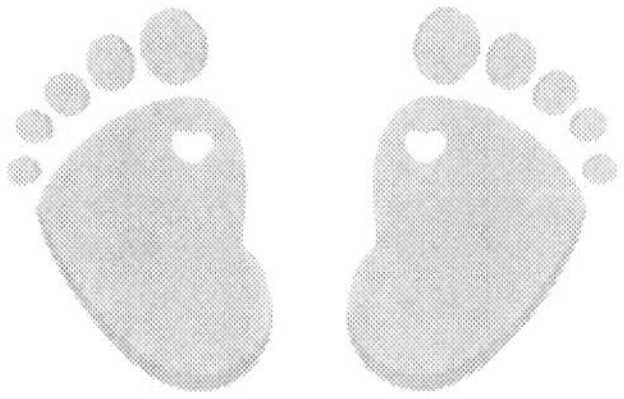

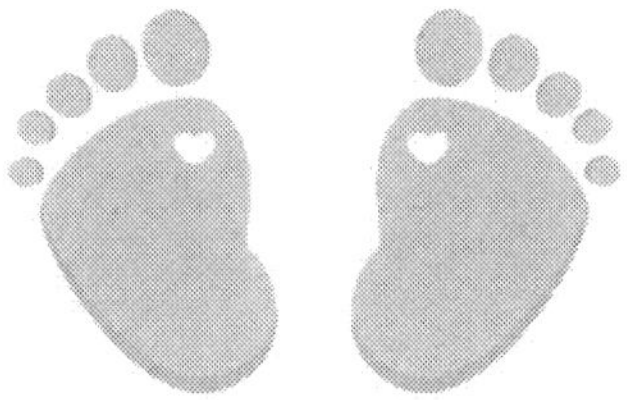

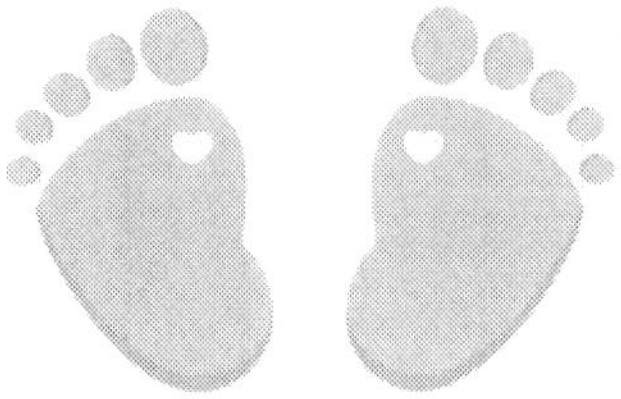

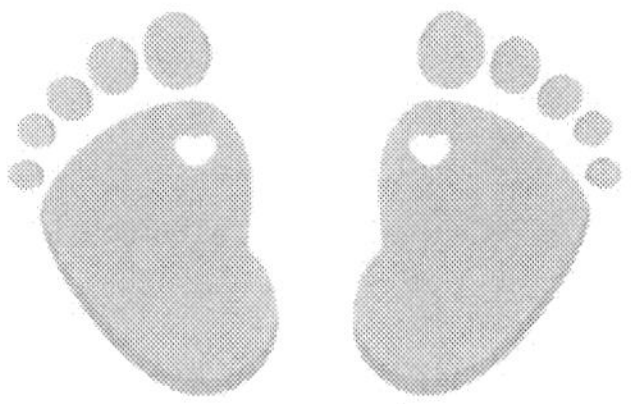

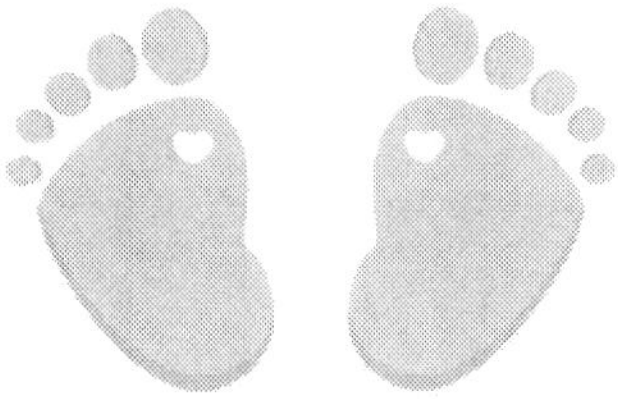

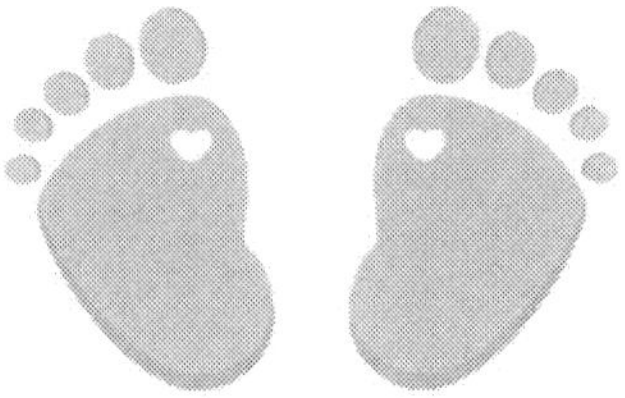

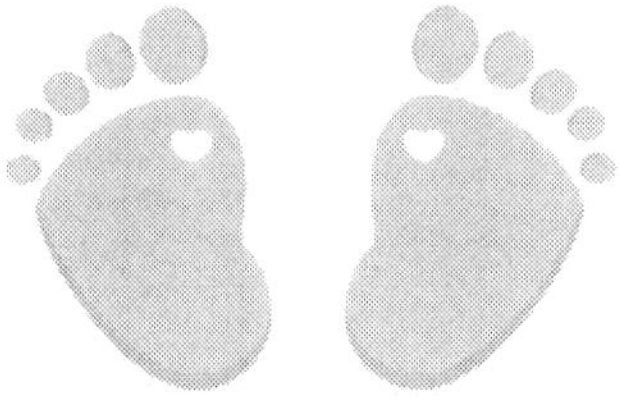

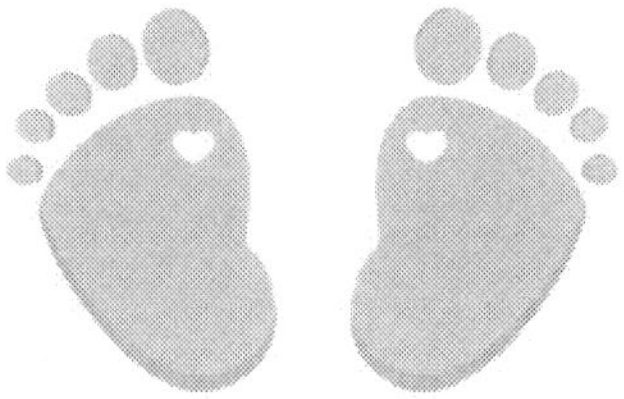

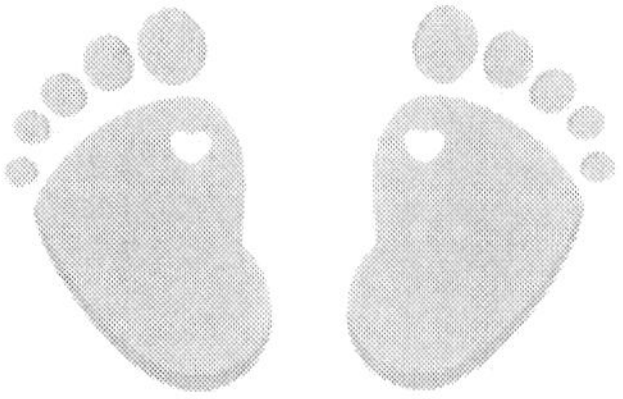

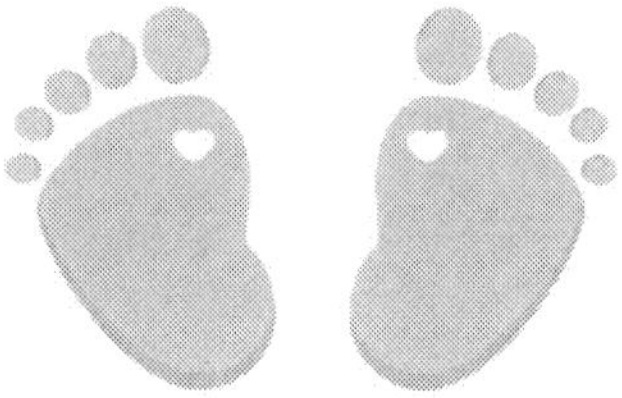

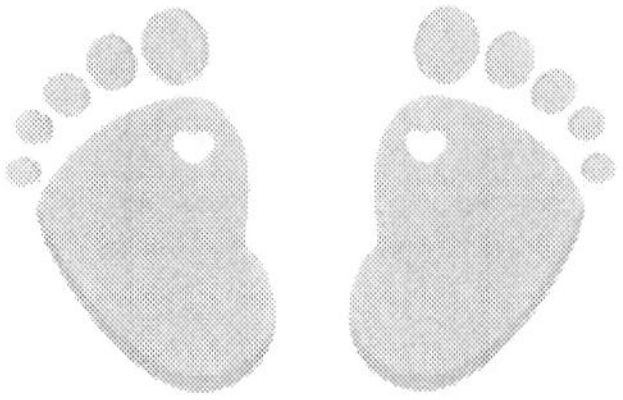

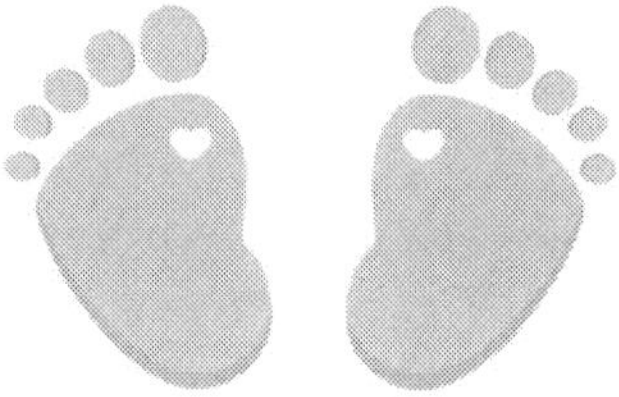

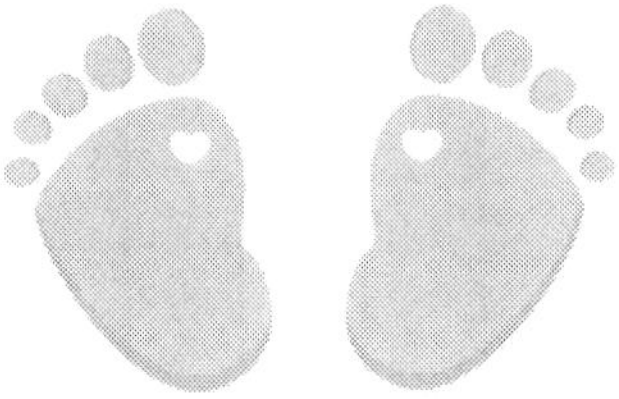

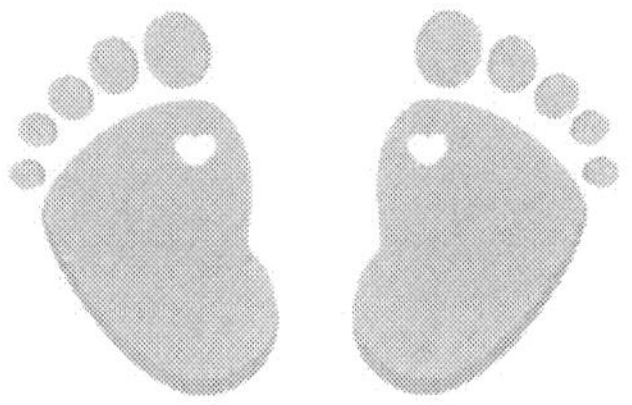

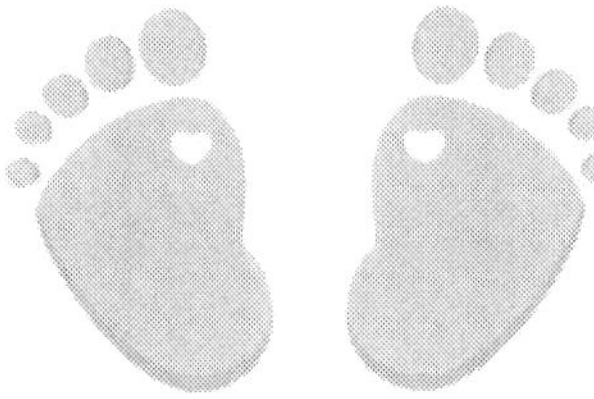

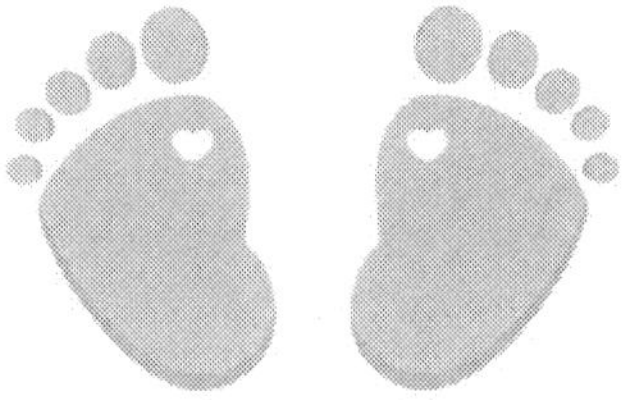

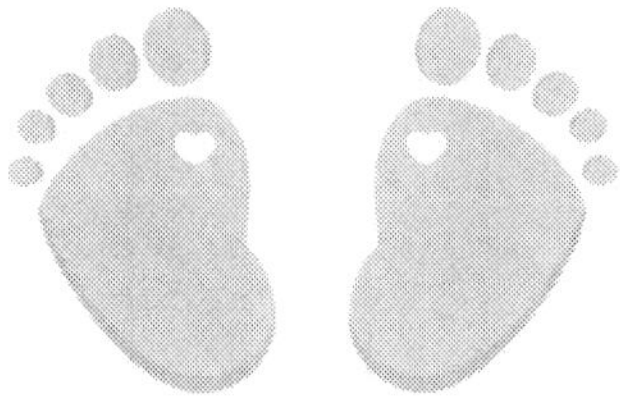

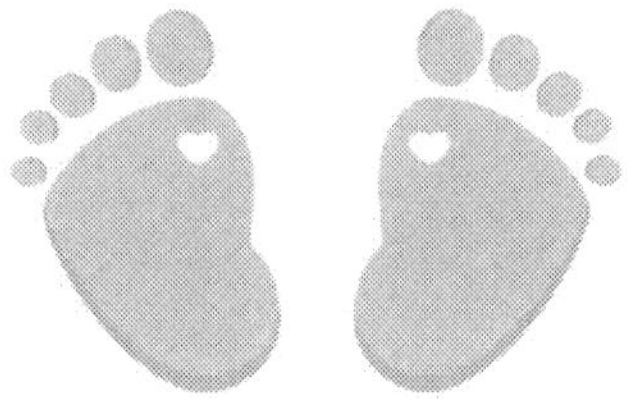

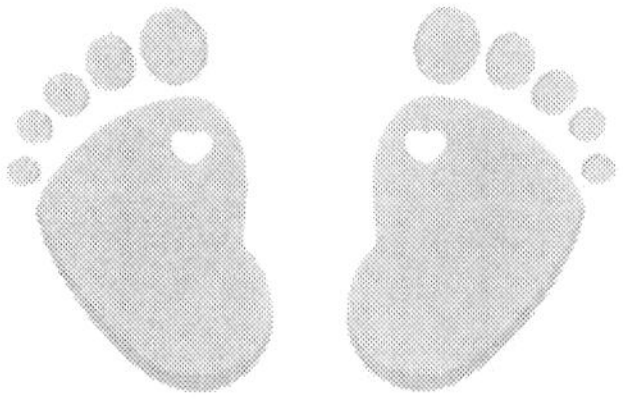

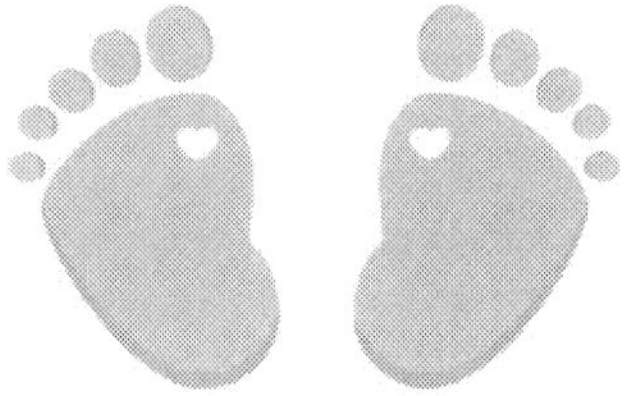

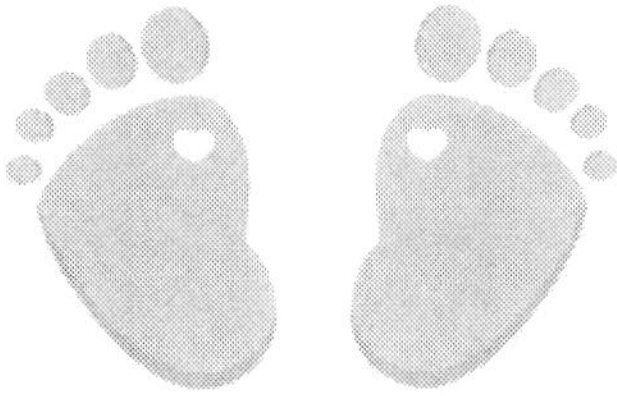

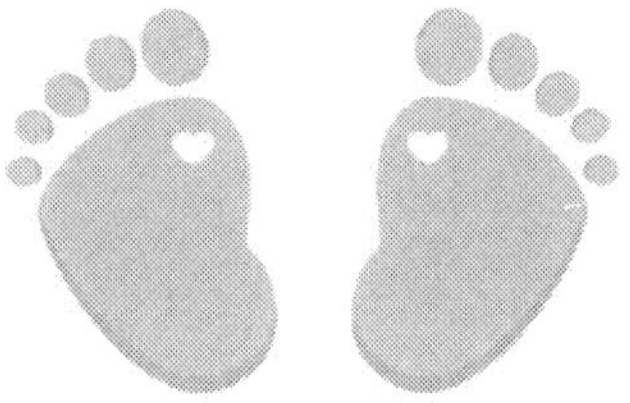

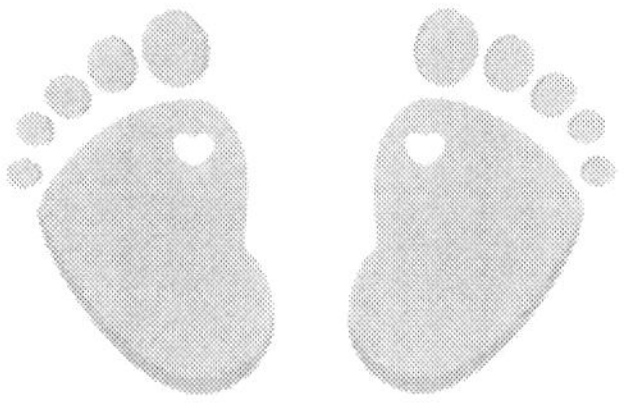

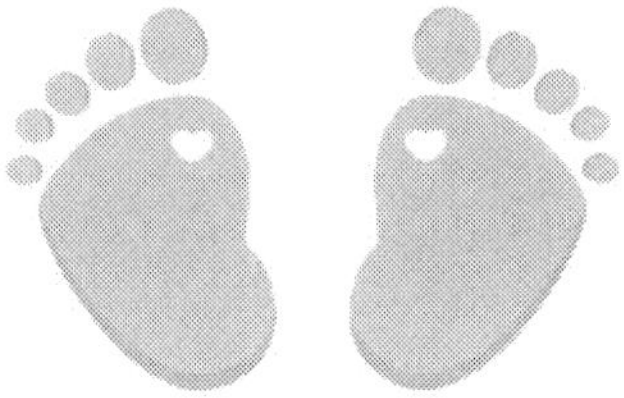

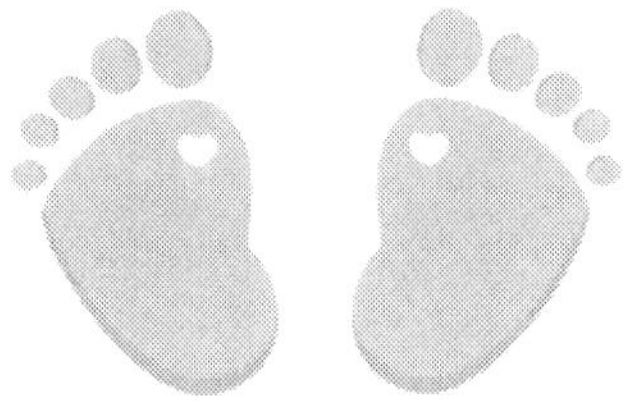

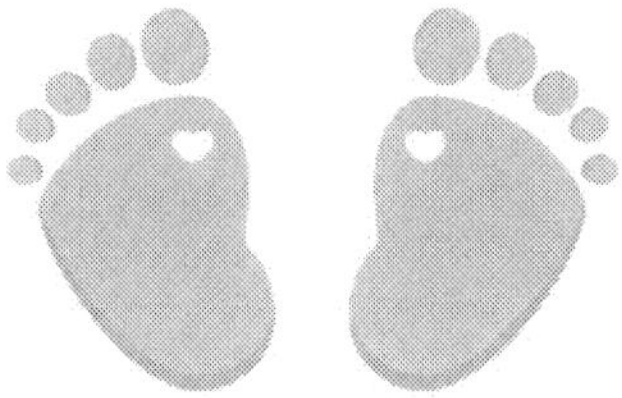

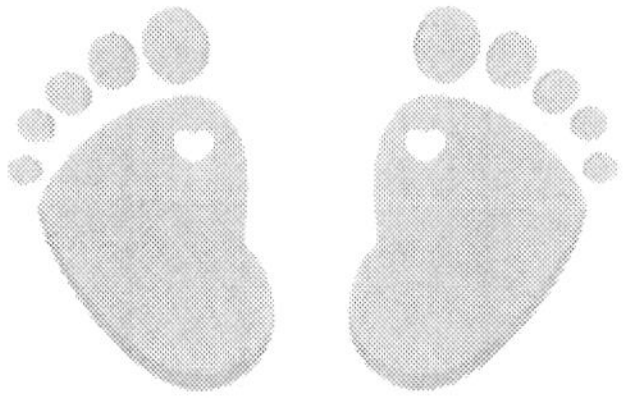

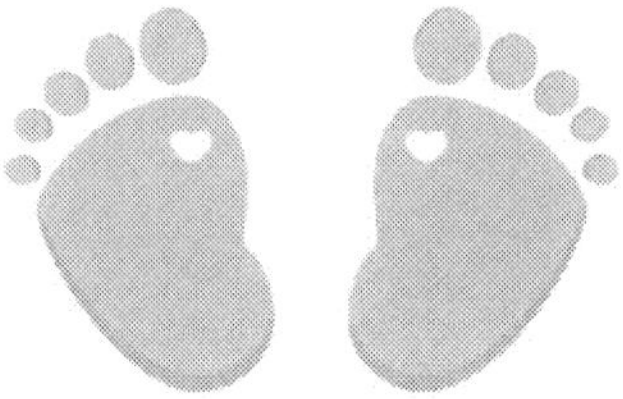

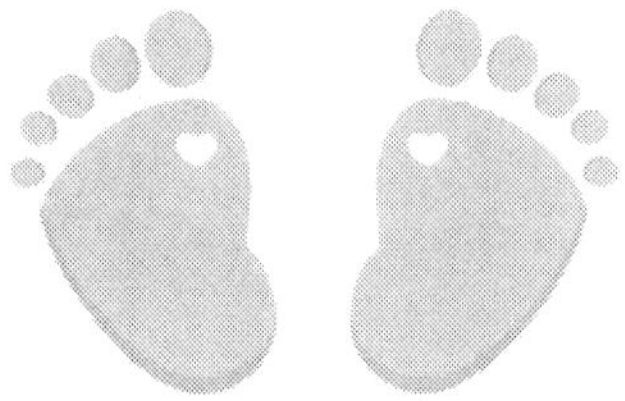

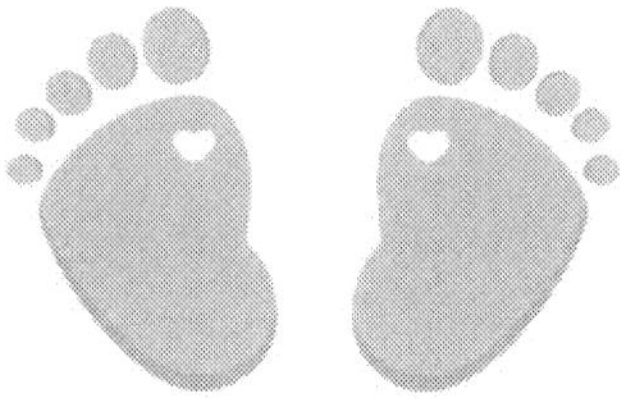

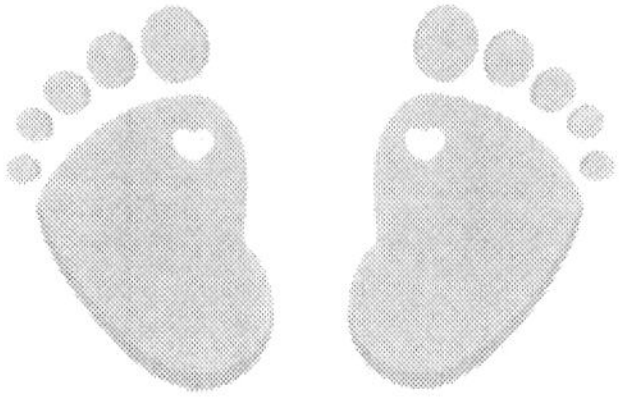

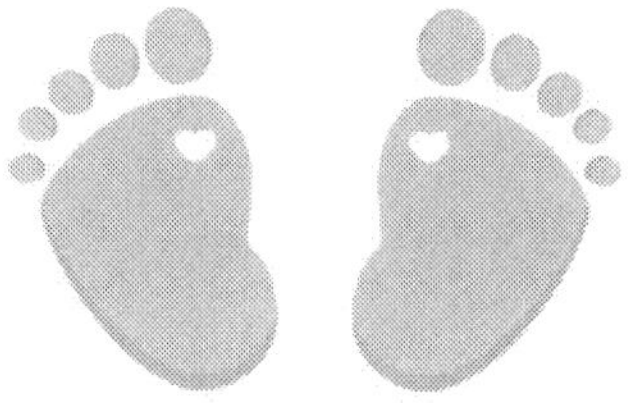

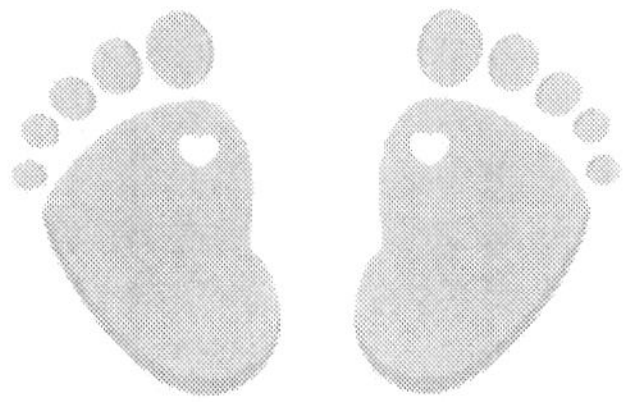

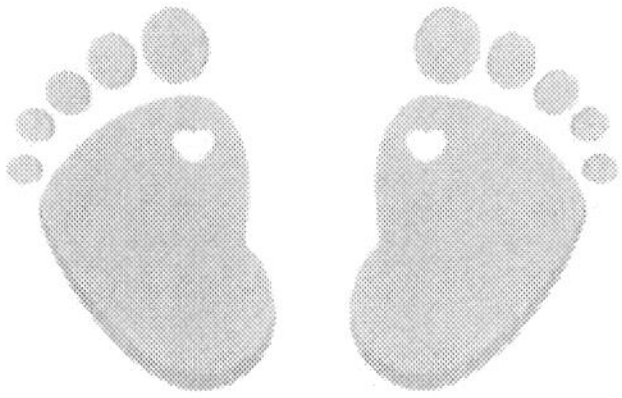

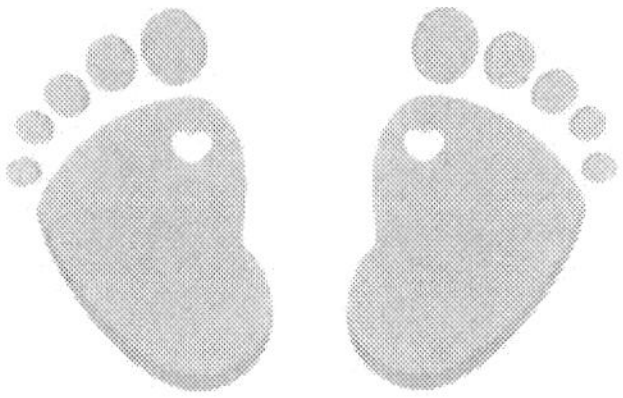

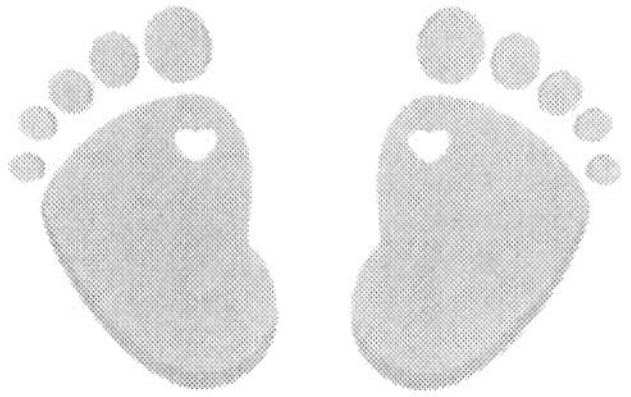

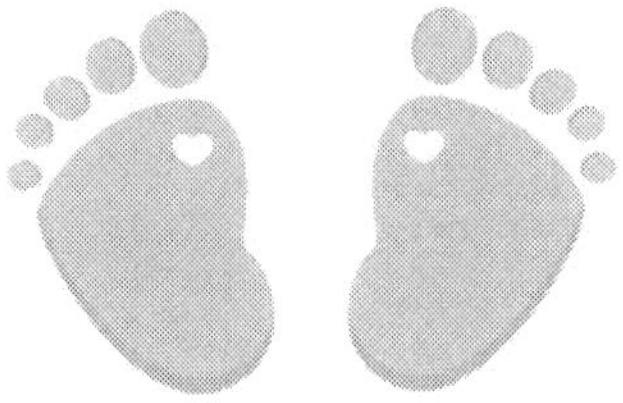

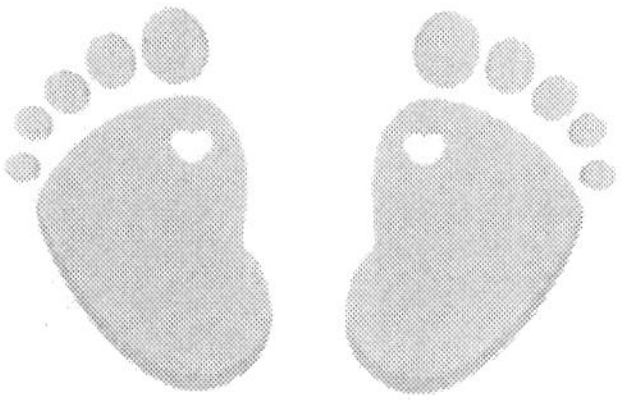

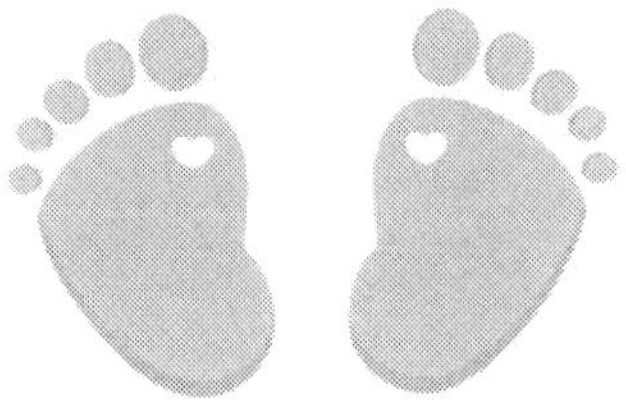

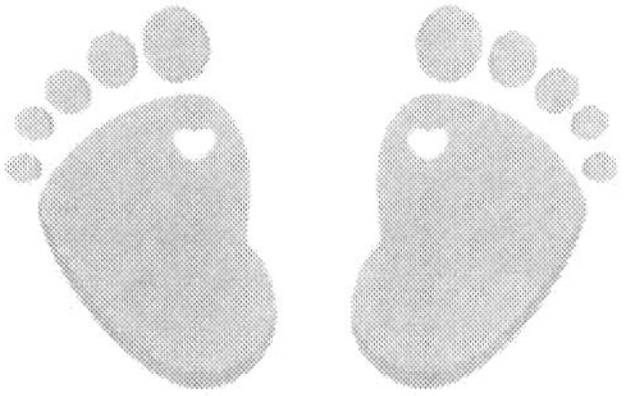

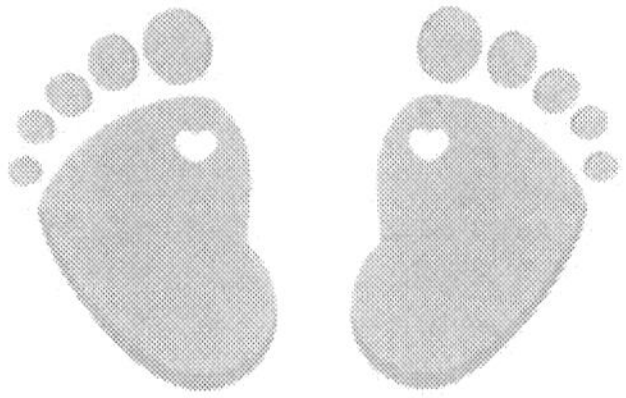

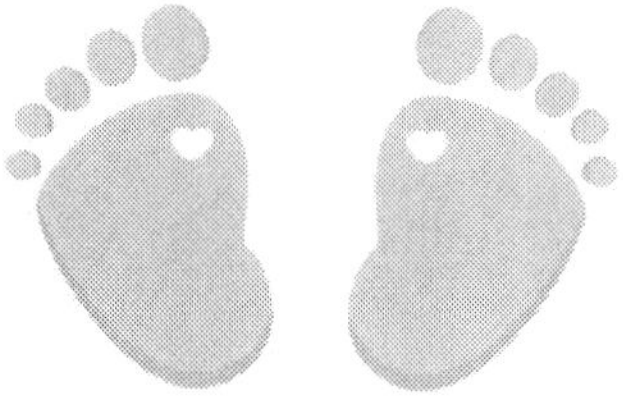

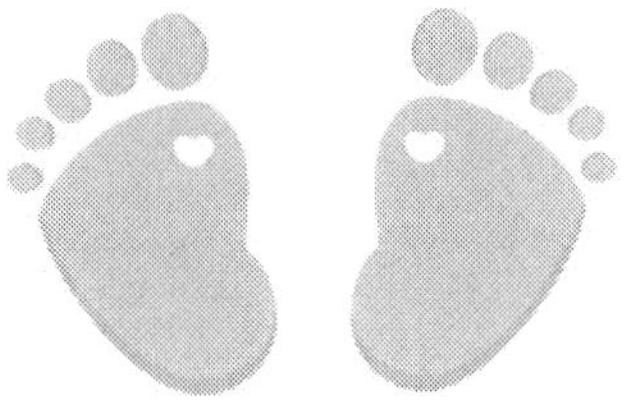

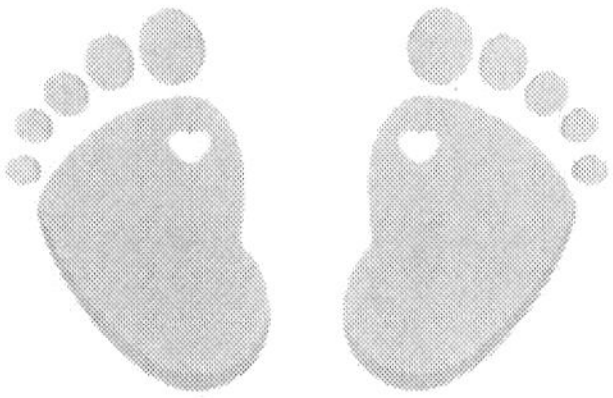

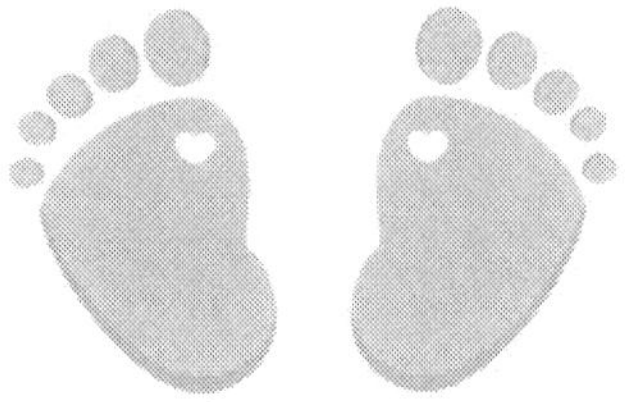

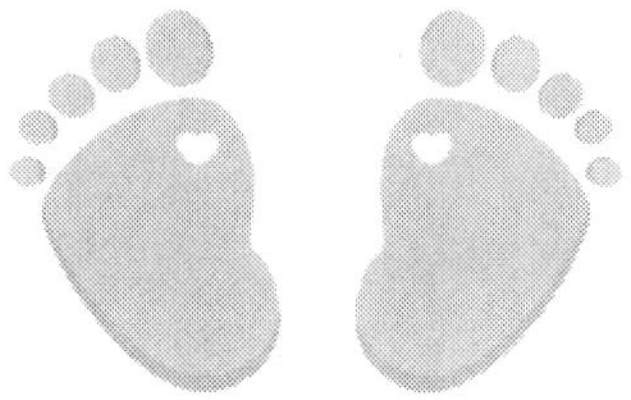

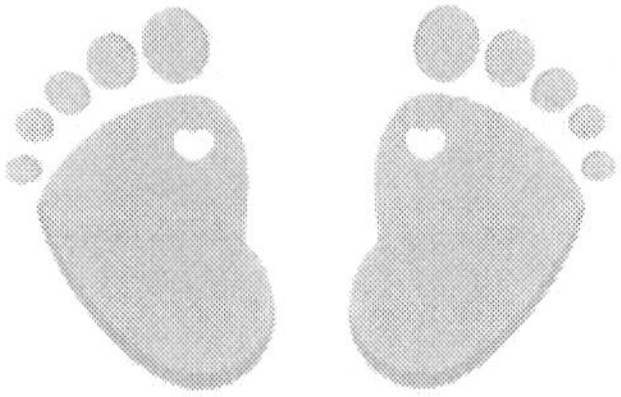

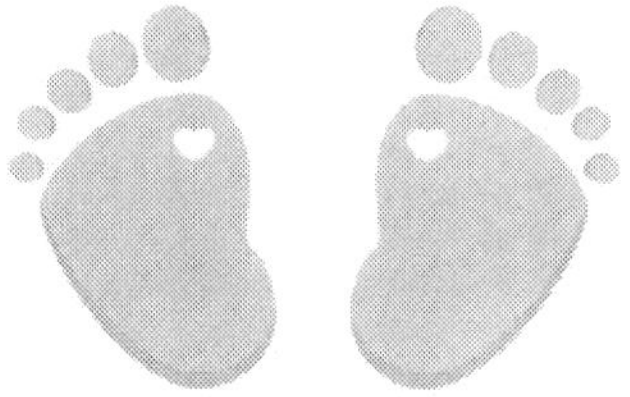

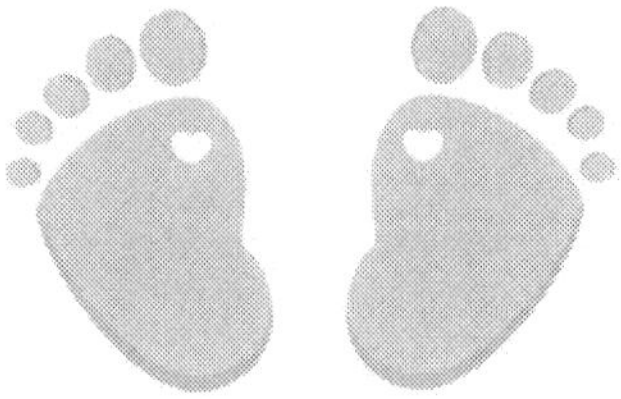

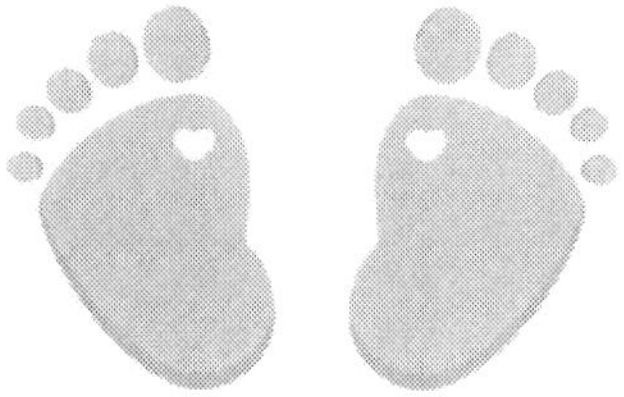

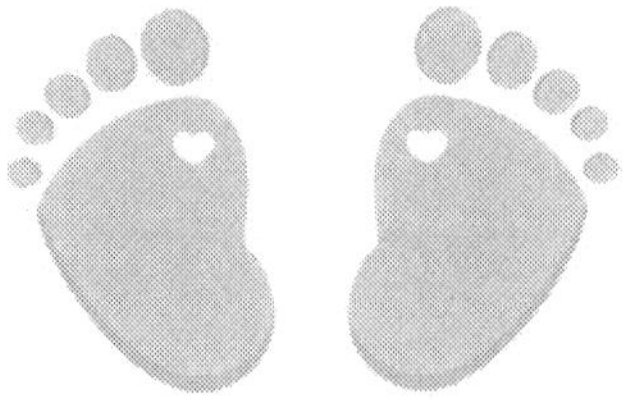

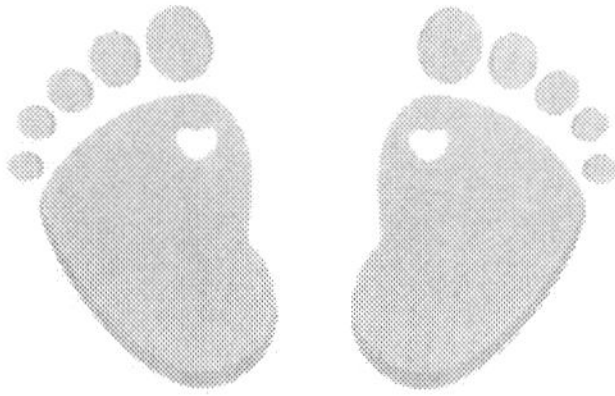

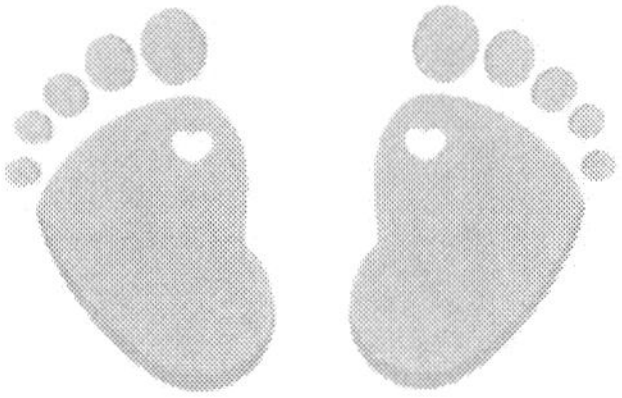

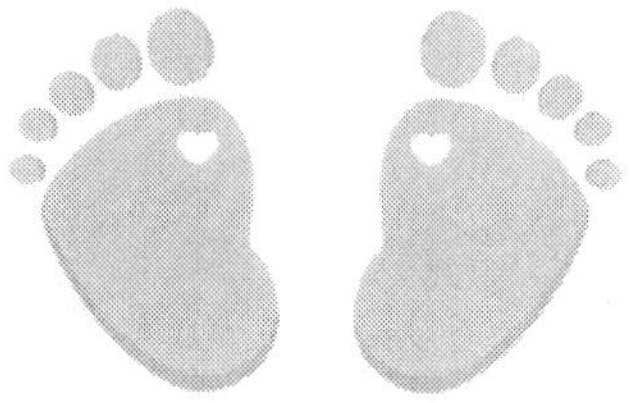

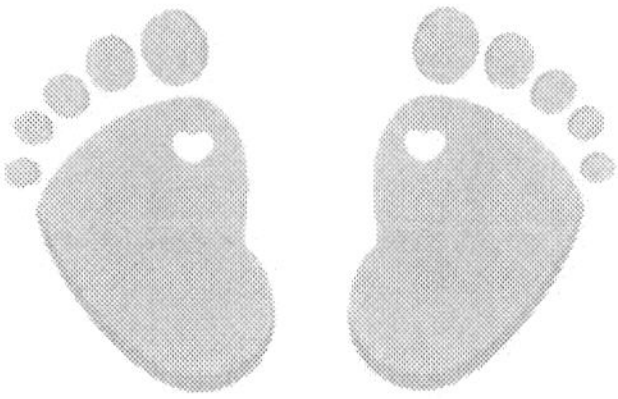

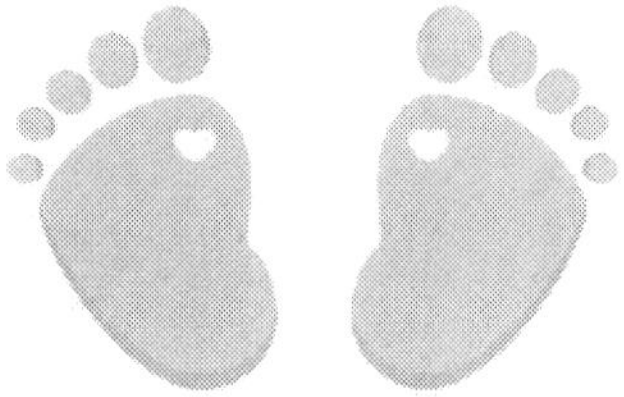

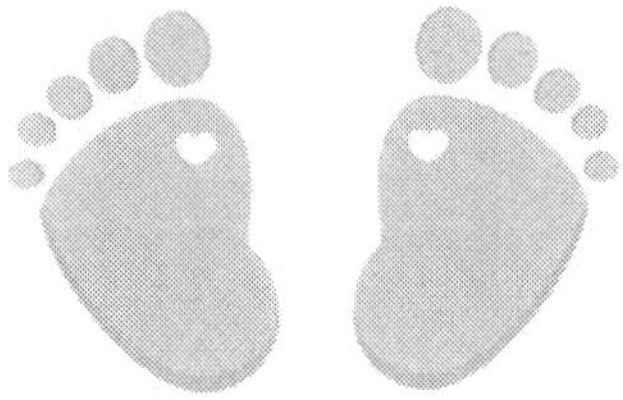

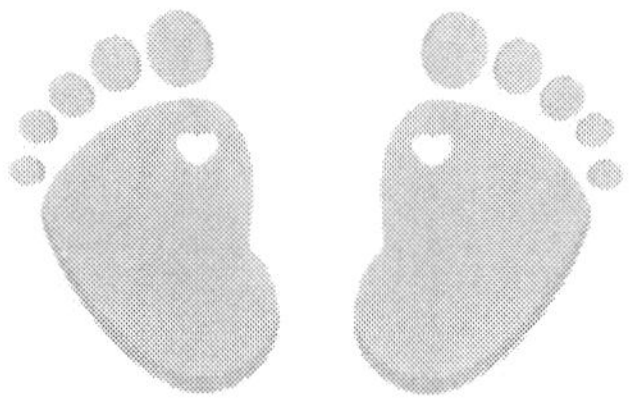

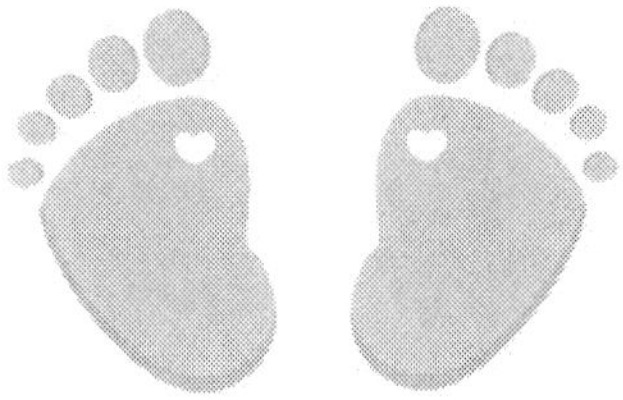

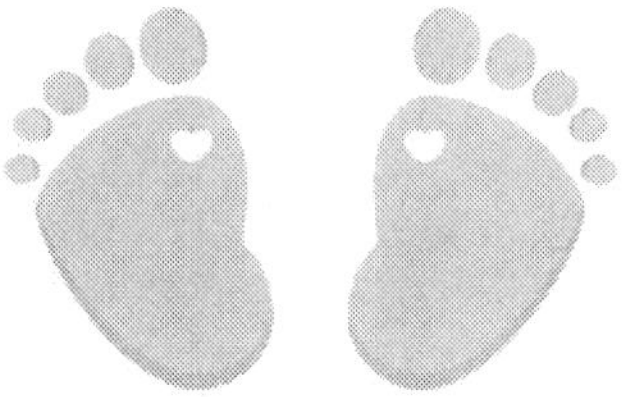

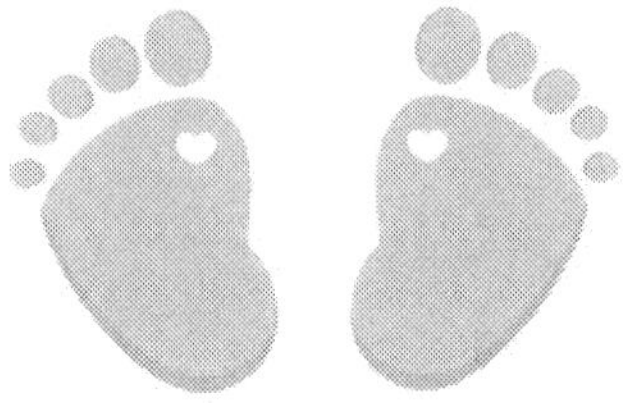

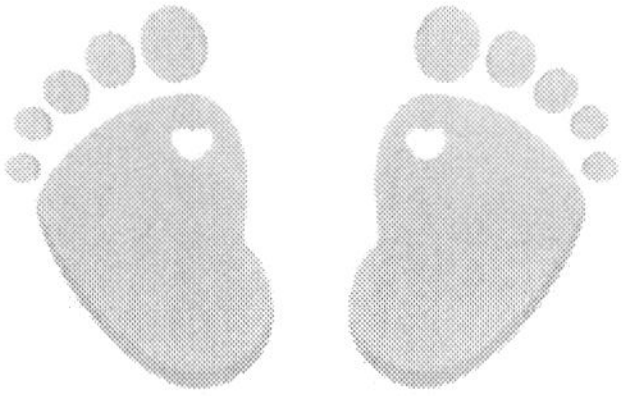

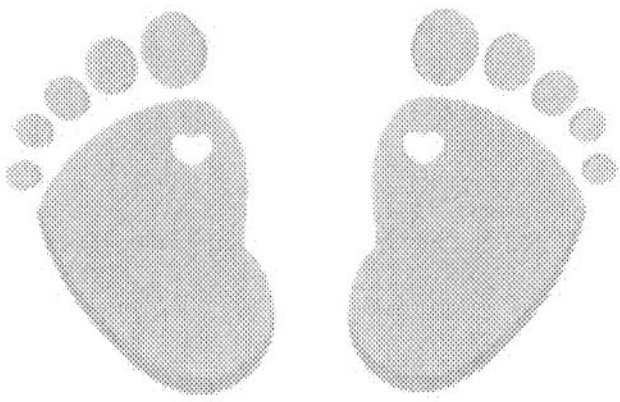

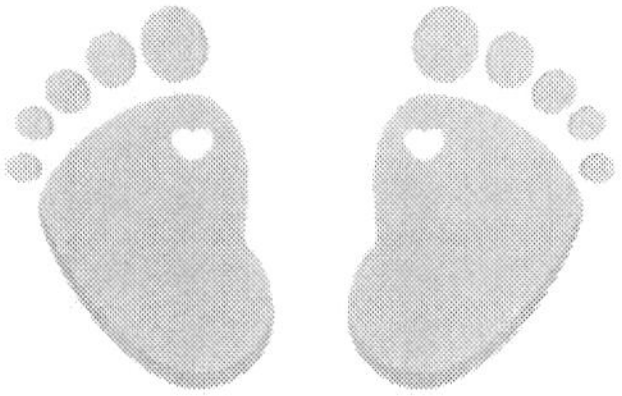

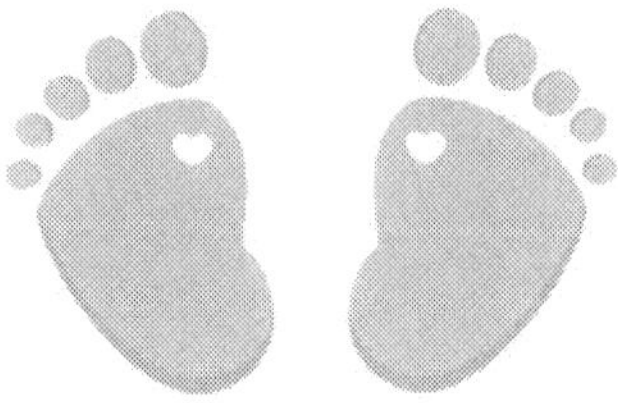

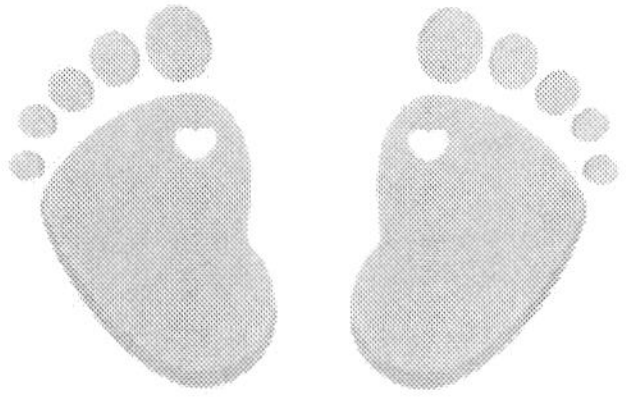

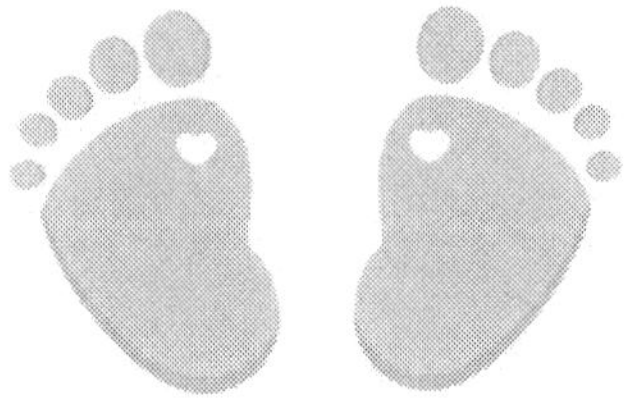

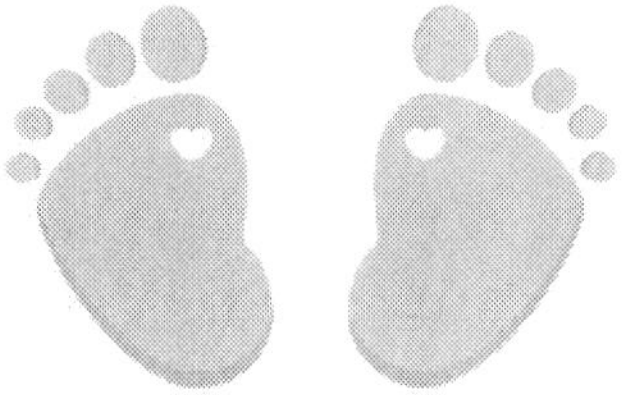

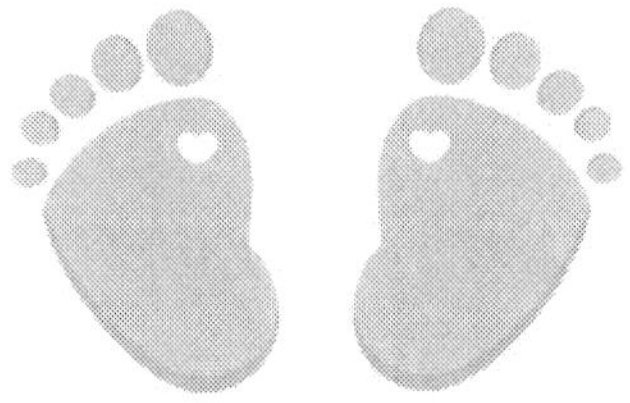

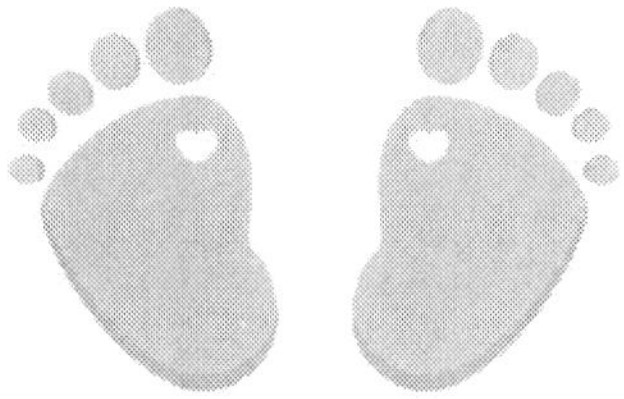

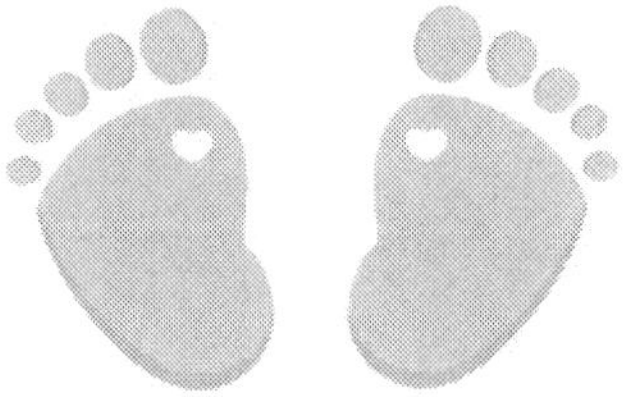

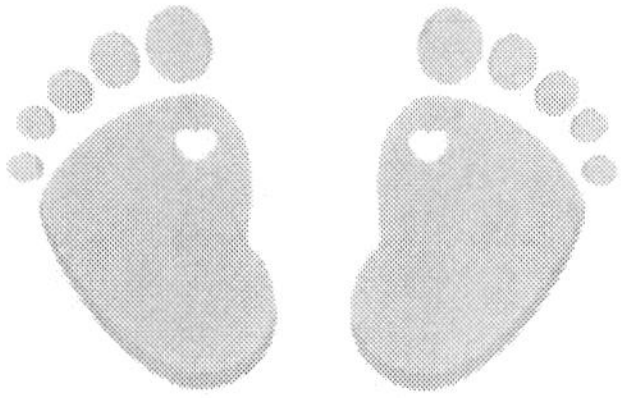

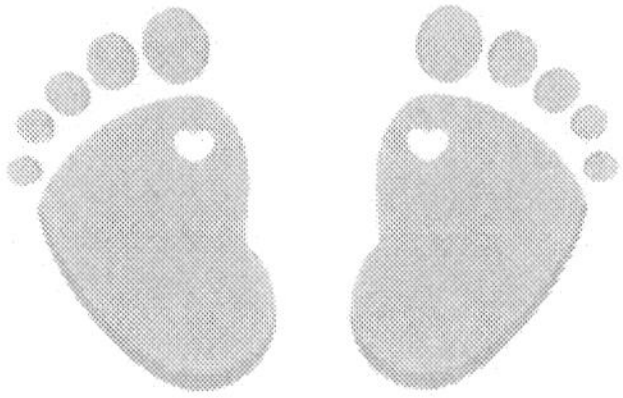

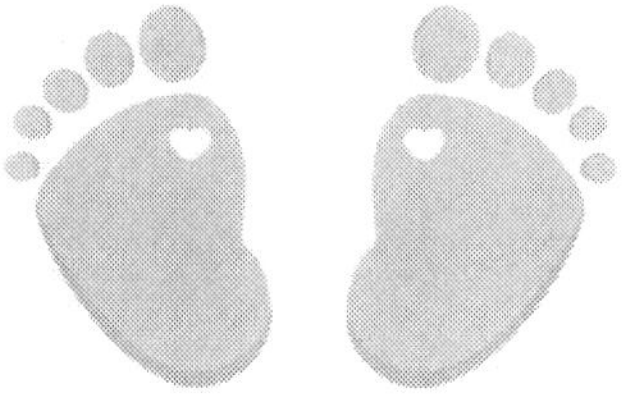

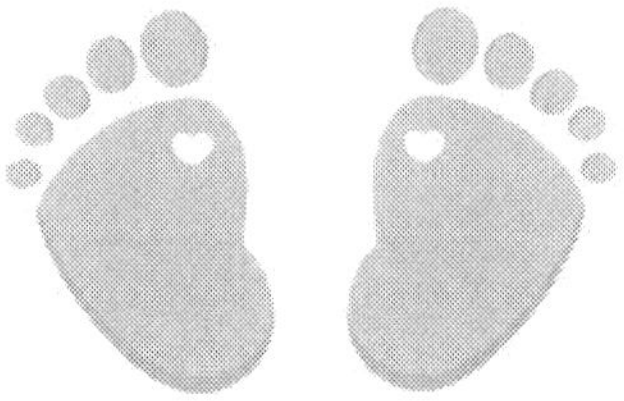

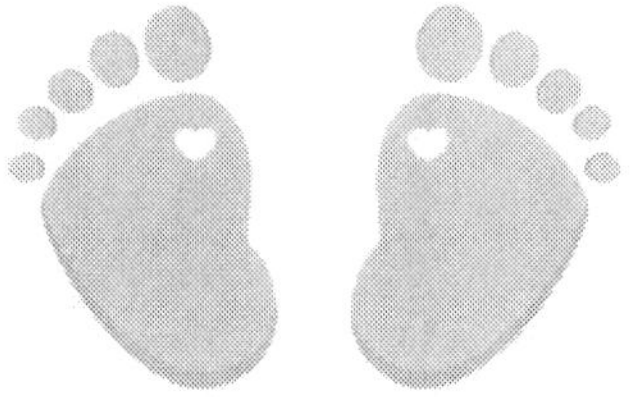

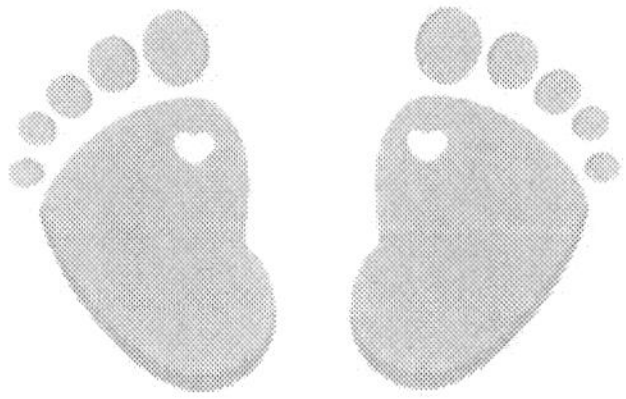

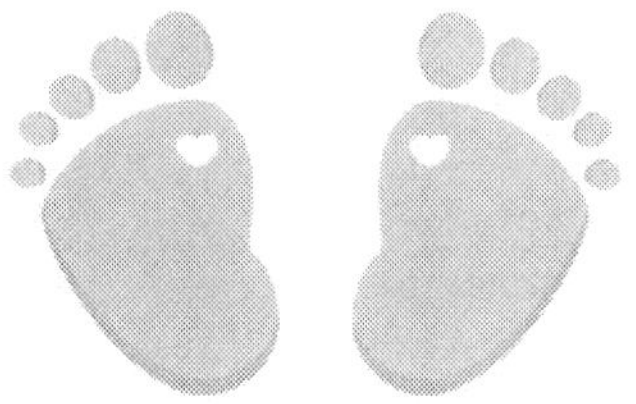

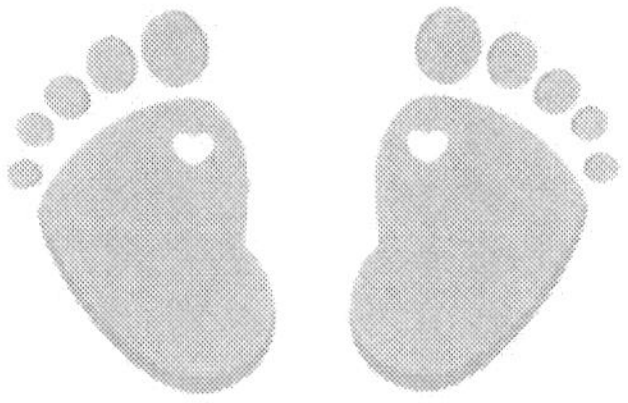

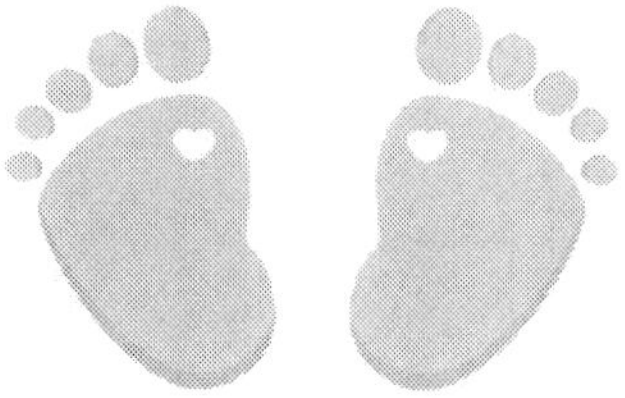

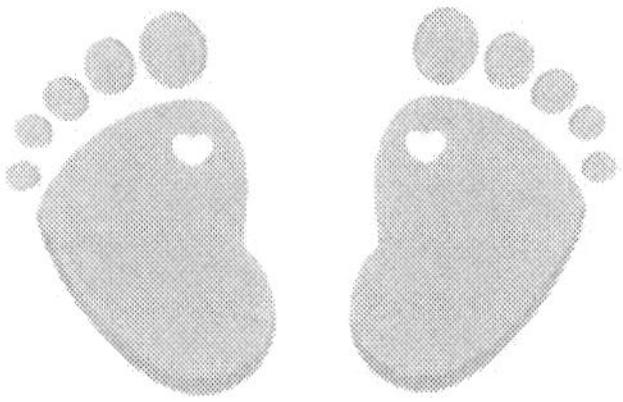

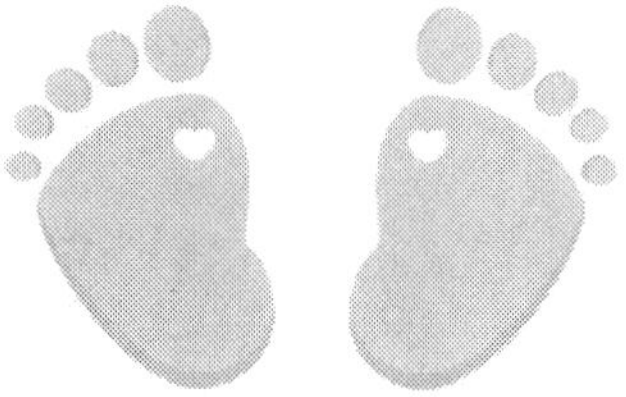

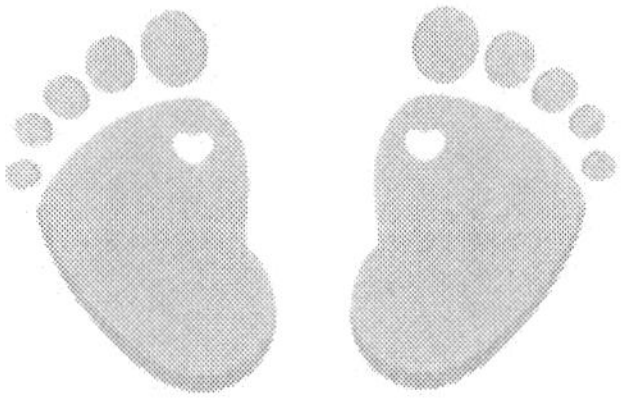

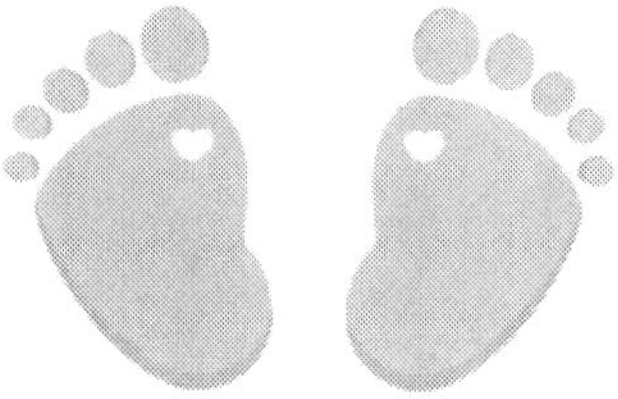

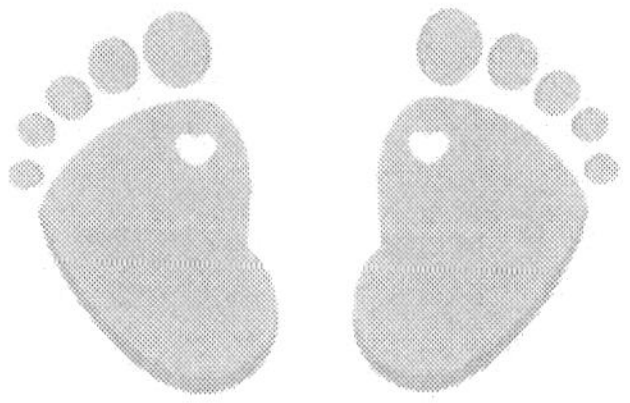

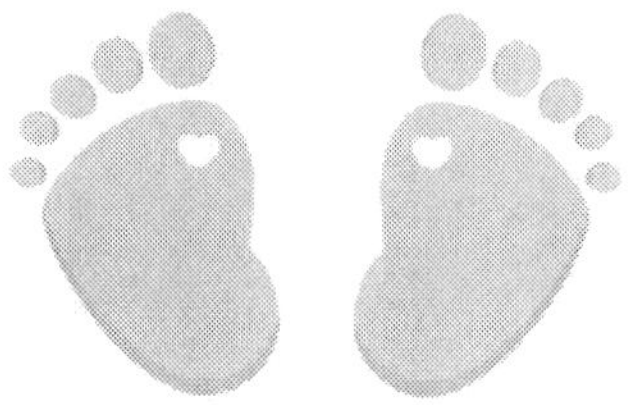

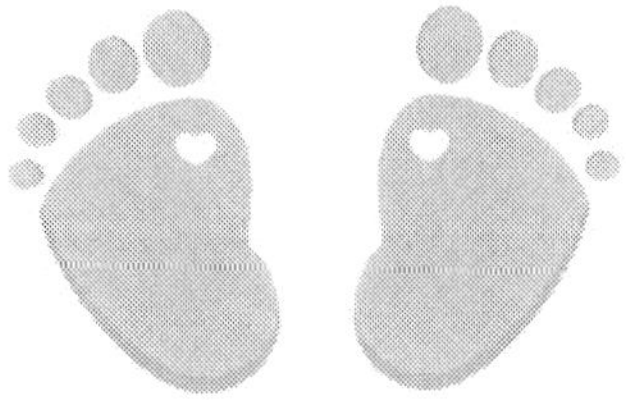

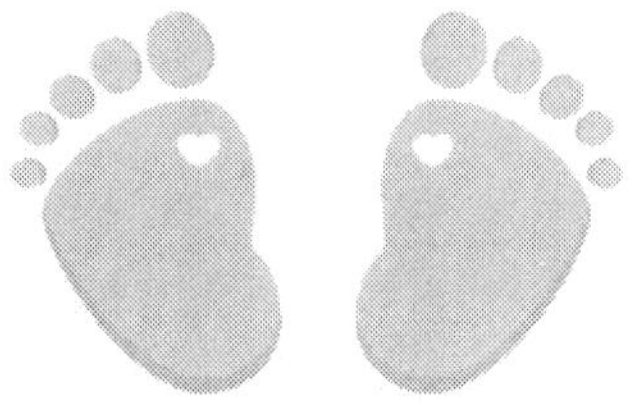

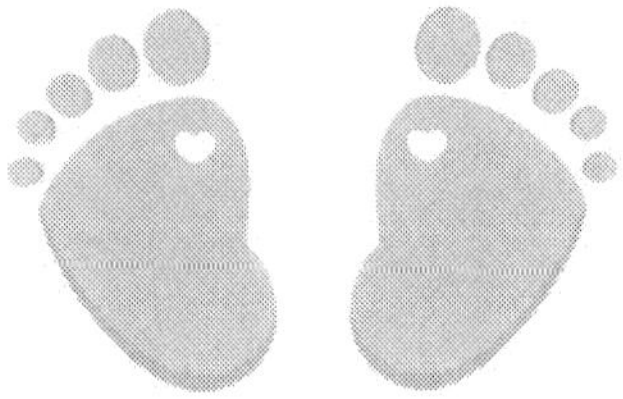

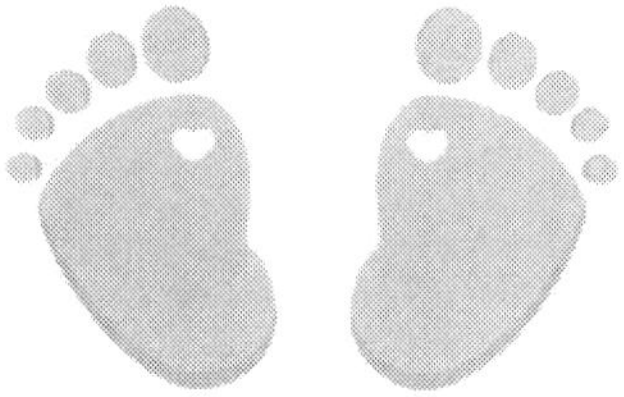

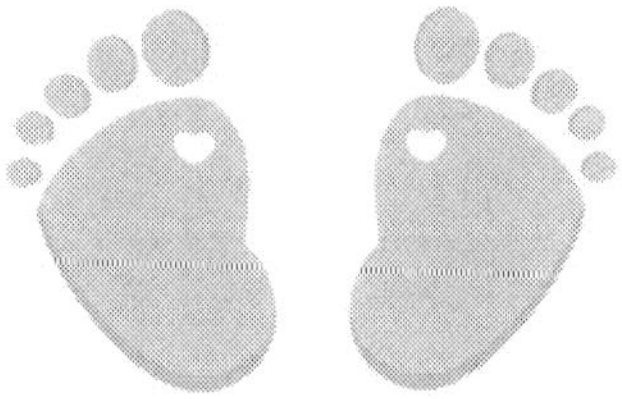

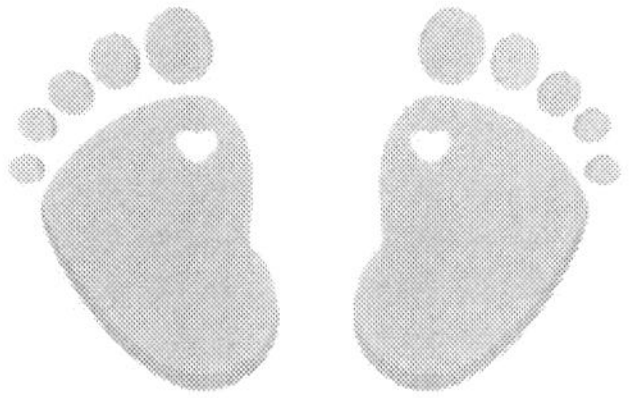

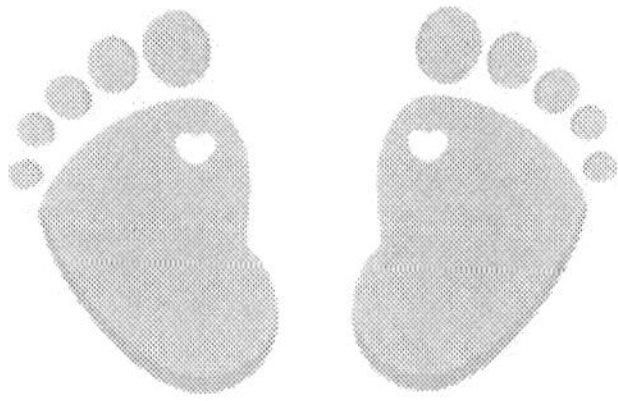

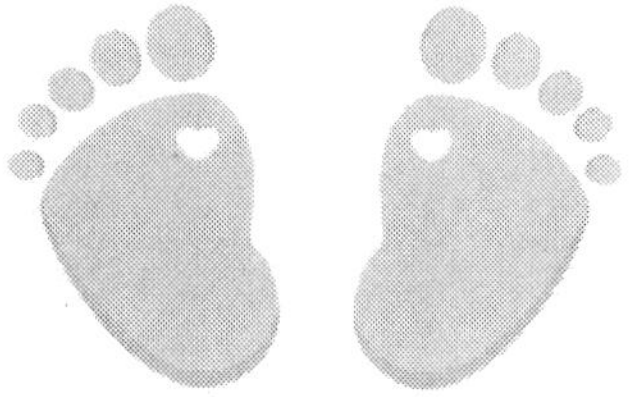

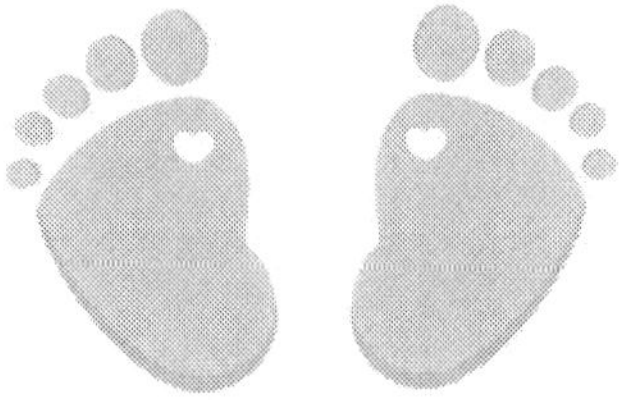

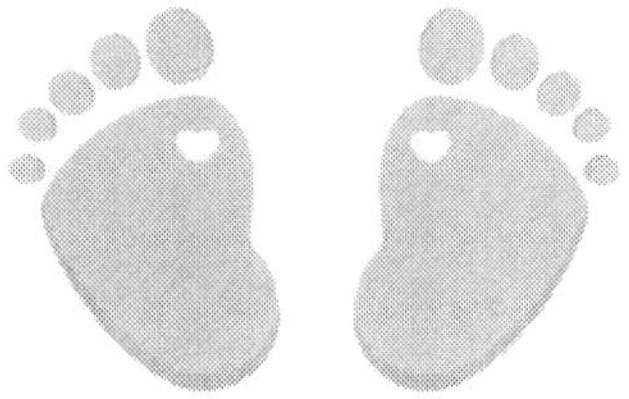

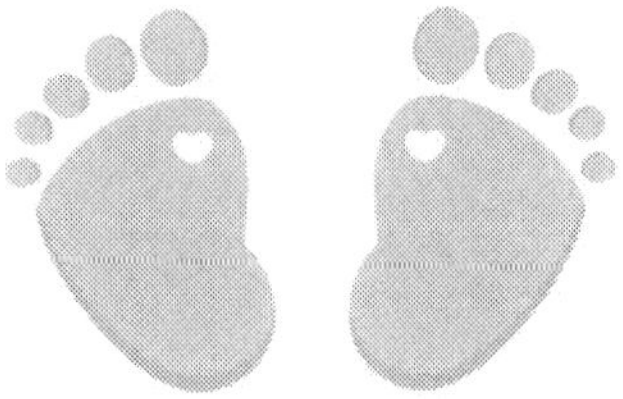

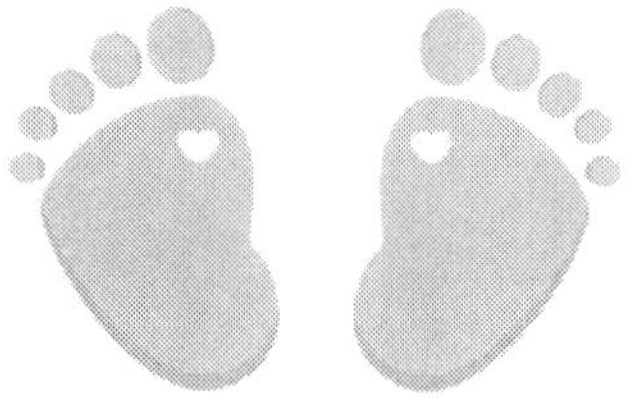

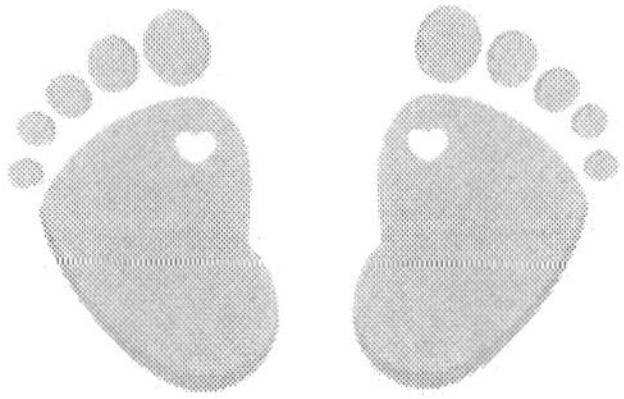

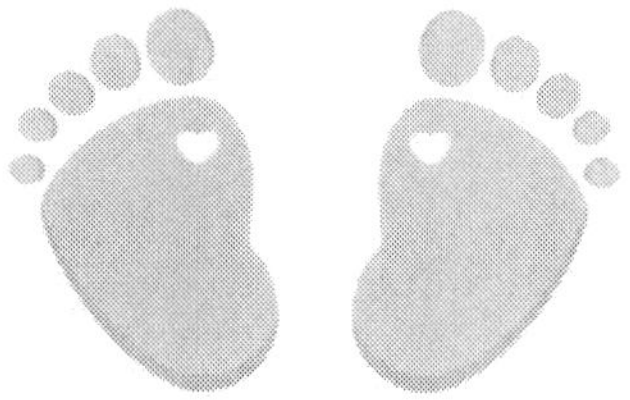

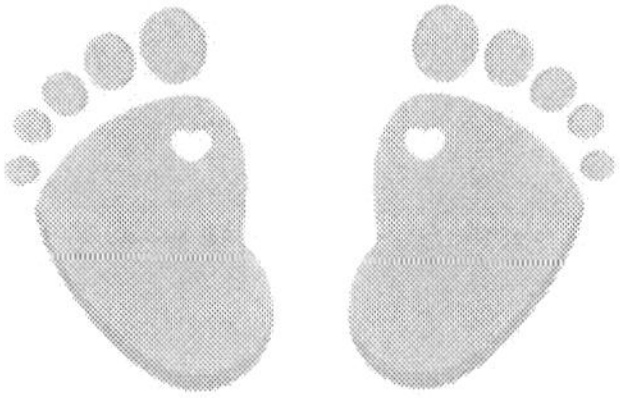

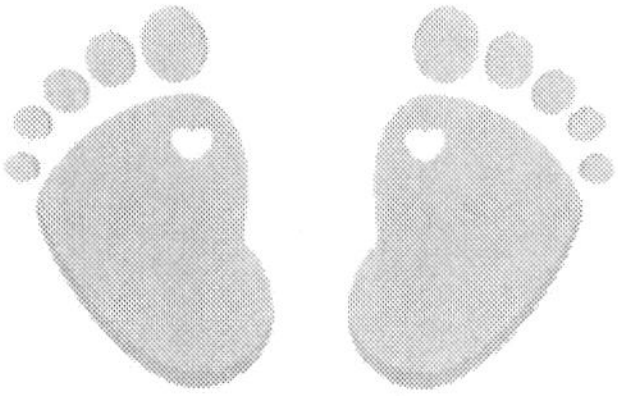

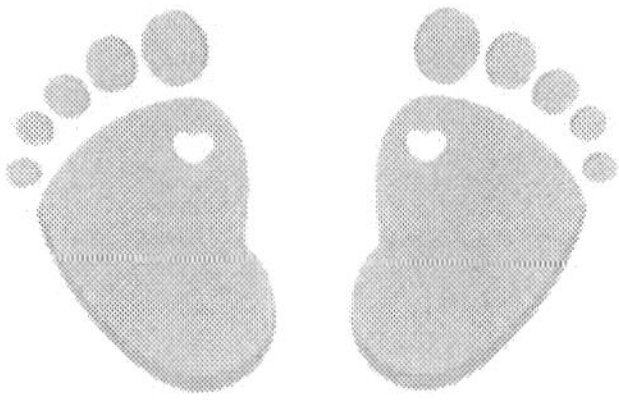

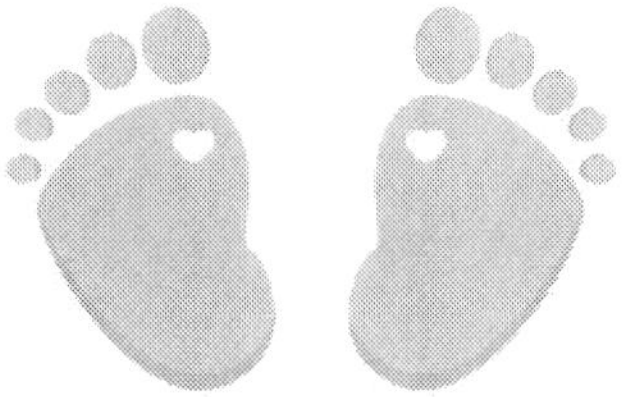

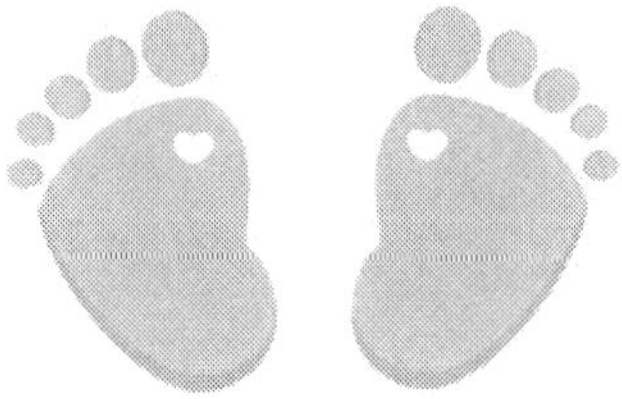

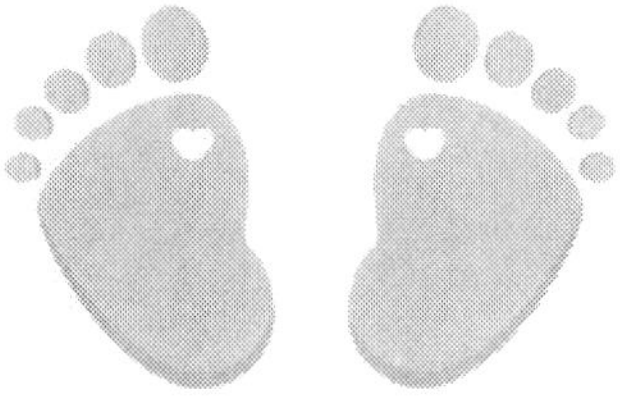

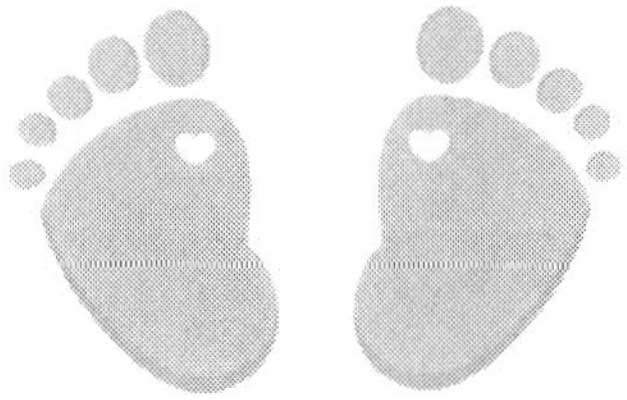

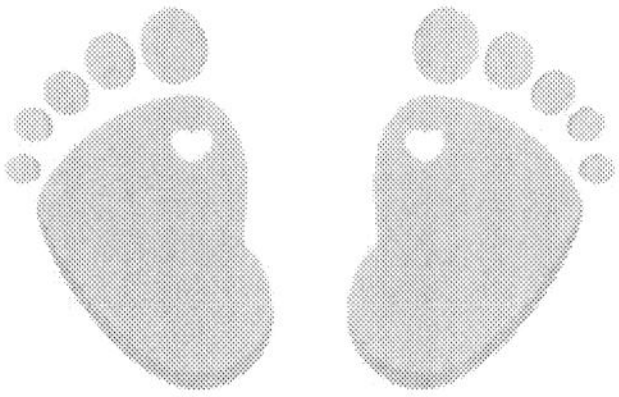

18086123R00084

Made in the USA
Middletown, DE
29 November 2018